TEACHING

HOw TO LEARN

TEACHING
HOW TO LEARN
The Teacher's Guide to Student Success

Kenneth A. Kiewra

Foreword by

William H. Peltz

CORWIN PRESS
A SAGE Company

For information:

Corwin Press
A SAGE Company
2455 Teller Road
Thousand Oaks, California 91320
www.corwinpress.com

SAGE Ltd.
1 Oliver's Yard
55 City Road
London EC1Y 1SP
United Kingdom

SAGE India Pvt. Ltd.
B 1/I 1 Mohan Cooperative
    Industrial Area
Mathura Road, New Delhi 110 044
India

SAGE Asia-Pacific Pte. Ltd.
33 Pekin Street #02-01
Far East Square
Singapore 048763

Printed in the United States of America

Library of Congress Cataloging-in-Publication Data

Kiewra, Kenneth A.
Teaching how to learn: The teacher's guide to student success/Kenneth A. Kiewra.
    p. cm.
Includes bibliographical references and index.
ISBN 978-1-4129-6533-0 (cloth)
ISBN 978-1-4129-6534-7 (pbk.)
    1. Teaching. 2. Academic achievement. I. Title.

LB1025.3.K554 2009
371.102—dc22   2008026492

This book is printed on acid-free paper.

08   09   10   11   12   10   9   8   7   6   5   4   3   2   1

Acquisitions Editor:	Carol Chambers Collins
Editorial Assistant:	Brett Ory
Production Editor:	Amy Schroller
Copy Editor:	Codi Bowman
Typesetter:	C&M Digitals (P) Ltd.
Proofreader:	Jeffrey Bryant
Indexer:	Judy Hunt
Cover Designer:	Rose Storey

Contents

Foreword

William H. Peltz

When I grew up, teachers seemed to assume that students were born knowing how to study and behaved as if successful study behaviors were inheritable traits. Students who weren't working up to their potential were treated as if their genes just needed to be activated. I remember teachers telling me I should work harder. I never knew what that trite phrase really meant, but I painted a grave expression on my face, nodded my head, and then walked out the classroom door, only to continue studying in my sloppy, ineffective ways. Some teachers told me that I was clearly an intelligent boy and capable of earning better grades, but they left it to me to divine how I might accomplish that elusive goal. I had some truly great teachers, but I cannot recall any of them ever giving me a single strategy that might have changed my behavior or improved my study techniques. For a long time, I was unfocused, unorganized, and often uninterested. Eventually, I stumbled on techniques that worked for me. When I became a teacher, I discovered my experience was not unique. Like me, few of my students had ever been taught how to study, and although they wanted to do well, many did not know how to approach their work. I quickly learned that to help my students master my discipline, I would also have to help them learn the requisite study techniques.

Teaching a subject, that is, packaging and dispensing the correct information, creating dynamic class activities, writing homework exercises, and designing tests and quizzes, is a comparatively easy task. What is more challenging is observing and diagnosing the learning characteristics of the students, engaging them in a truly motivating dialogue, and helping them develop the learning skills that will give them optimum success. Not many teachers retool their class presentations in order to introduce and reinforce learning strategies. Regardless how difficult it might be, I believe opening this particular door and helping students learn how to learn should be central to all teaching. Enabling students to become self-aware, independent learners should be a central component of every teacher's professional mission statement.

For this reason, I am very excited by Kenneth Kiewra's *Teaching How to Learn*. He is not intent on simply providing a few study tips and tricks. Instead, he gives his readers a well thought out progression of strategies that do nothing less than help all students SOAR to success, an acronym he created to help the reader remember the basic steps of his model. Dr. Kiewra has a wonderful and humane vision: to empower all students so that they become any time, any place learners. He does not just focus on the student, however. His goal is to help every teacher become optimally effective so that learning is maximized. He shows teachers how to design instructional techniques that work synergistically with the child who is learning how to learn.

I enjoyed reading *Teaching How to Learn*. It is filled with anecdotes that engage the reader. Dr. Kiewra includes just enough research to make his points, but not so much that the book risks being dry and uninteresting. His sense of humor and light, engaging style made me feel I was sitting down with a colleague and friend, having a professional conversation in which I was the beneficiary. Dr. Kiewra knows how kids learn and what the teacher can do to help them learn more effectively, and he shares his expertise with a passion for teaching and an obvious compassion for the children who study in our schools. He offers multiple examples of the strategies that he describes so that we teachers can help our students grow into empowered, confident learners. This book is both insightful and helpful.

Teaching How to Learn starts with a bold statement. It claims that our schools fail because they focus too narrowly on course content and skills. By neglecting to teach students how to learn, schools deny most students the opportunity to achieve their maximum potential. Dr. Kiewra makes it quite clear that study skill teaching is not to be confused with remediation and that these skills are not something that students learn naturally as they move up in grade levels. He understands that many teachers do not create an ideal learning environment simply because they themselves were not taught how to learn. He deserves much praise, therefore, because he shares the techniques that can rectify this problem. His goal is to improve instruction so that students can soar, and I believe he succeeds magnificently. Professor Kiewra offers a carefully laid out model, and now it is up to us teachers to implement it.

This book should be read by anyone who wants to grow as an educator and who strives to become a master teacher. It should be required reading for the teacher who cares deeply for the total growth, success, and happiness of every child in the classroom. *Teaching How to Learn* should occupy a place in the professional library of every teacher, new or seasoned veteran, and should be found in every faculty lounge. I hope you enjoy it!

Preface

Suppose you were to teach students the following information about the appearance of spiders and insects. How would you go about it?

Spiders have two body parts: the head and chest. They have eight legs and eight eyes. They do not have wings or antennae. Their skeleton is a hard outer shell that protects them.

A hard outer shell protects an insect's three body parts: head, chest, and abdomen. They usually have two big eyes and three smaller eyes between them. Six legs and one or two pairs of wings propel insects. Insects also have a pair of antennae for sensing things.

Simply giving students these blocks of information to learn is not the ticket. Most students employ weak learning strategies. Teachers can foster learning by helping students **select, organize, associate**, and **regulate** lesson information. When teachers do, they help students SOAR to success. Moreover, teachers can teach students SOAR strategies so they can learn effectively anytime, anyplace. Let's take a look.

Select

Spiders

Body Parts: 2, Head and chest

Legs: 8

Eyes: 8

Wings: None

Antennae: None

Skeleton: Hard outer shell

Insects

Skeleton: Hard outer shell

Body Parts: 3, Head, chest, and abdomen

Eyes: 2 big and 3 smaller between them

Legs: 6

Wings: 1 or 2 pairs

Antennae: 1 pair

Organize

	Spiders	*Insects*
Skeleton	Hard outer shell	Hard outer shell
Body Parts	2: head, chest	3: head, chest, abdomen
Eyes	8	2 big, 3 small between
Legs	8	6
Wings	no	1–2 pairs
Antennae	no	1 pair

Associate

- Both have hard outer shells.
- Spiders have 8 eyes and 8 legs. Think of a spider like a table where each corner has 2 legs and each side has 2 eyes.
- Spiders have no wings or antennae. Think about Spiderman who had no wings or antennae.
- Both have heads and chests, but only the insect has an abdomen. Think about a bee (insect) with a fat belly.
- Insects have fewer eyes (5) than spiders (8) but compensate by having antennae to sense things.
- Insects have fewer legs (6) than spiders (8) but compensate by having wings for flight.

Regulate

Answer spider, insect, or both.

1. Wings
2. Three body parts

3. Hard outer shell

4. Eight legs and eyes

5.

6.

Strategy Instruction

"Class, I gave you a chart comparing spiders and insects that helped you organize lesson information. The chart showed at a glance what the paragraphs could not show: similarities and differences between spiders and insects. The chart showed that both have hard outer shells; insects have more body parts than spiders, and have wings and antennae whereas spiders do not. Spiders, meanwhile, have more eyes and legs than insects. Creating a chart is an effective and useful strategy anytime you want to compare information and learn relationships. You'll get a chance to practice when we later create a chart to compare various spiders and one to compare various insects."

From this example, you can see that effective instructors do more than toss out information for students to learn. They teach in ways that ensure student learning and teach students *how* to learn. Teacher A is my name for those who teach in ways that ensure learning, and Teacher

A+ is my name for those who instruct like Teacher A *plus* teach strategies for how to learn.

Students need A and A+ teachers. Without them, many students are ineffective learners—even college students who note just 35% of important lesson points, organize those points in hapless lists and outlines, and study isolated facts using redundant strategies like re-copying, rereading, and reciting . . . ridiculous! Instead, students should use effective strategies that help them soar to success. They should select and note all the important lesson information; organize it using representations, instead of lists and outlines; associate the information so that meaningful relationships are learned rather than just isolated facts; and regulate learning by generating and answering testlike problems rather than employ redundant strategies. Unfortunately, students are not likely to learn this way unless Teacher A presents material in ways that foster SOAR strategies or unless Teacher A+ teaches students SOAR strategies that equip them to soar to success anytime, anywhere.

This book prepares you to teach like Teachers A and A+. Part I introduces you to the SOAR teaching system. It presents and models techniques you can use to foster and teach selection, organization, association, and regulation strategies. Part II covers three supporting topics: motivation, behavior management, and talent development. Here's why. Students cannot soar to success unless they are also motivated and in control of behavior. And, when all systems are go, talent can soar to extraordinary heights.

The focus of this book—helping students soar to success—makes it useful for all teachers, from those just starting out in teacher education programs to those with untold experience. It's appropriate for those in elementary, secondary, and post secondary education and across disciplines from art to zoology. And it's appropriate too for those who teach outside school boundaries such as coaches, club leaders, and parents. If you want practical, hands-on advice on how to help students soar to success, this book is for you.

Acknowledgments

I appreciate the many people who influenced and shaped *Teaching How to Learn.*

Perhaps most influential were the A+ teachers who taught me along the way: committed and skilled educators like Mr. Coddington who taught difficult science material using clever and amusing associations; Ms. Williams, an English teacher, who taught me to let my ideas out—within the confines of grammatical rules of course; Mr. O'Donnell, a social studies teacher, who somehow made history contemporary; Dr. DuBois, a college professor, whose captivating style and passion for teaching and learning made me want to be an educational psychologist just like him; and Dr. Fletcher, the most stringent and helpful mentor a graduate student could hope to find. Not only did they model A+ teaching, they motivated me to teach from the bottom of my heart.

I am also indebted to longtime colleagues for all they taught me about learning and instruction. Thank you Dr. Stephen Benton (Kansas State University), Dr. Richard Mayer (University of California, Santa Barbara), and Dr. Joel Levin (University of Arizona). Your knowledge and teaching are inspiring.

Many current and former students helped shape my ideas as well. They include Maribeth Christensen, Dave Christian, Patti Gubbels, Brent Igo, Dharma Jairam, Doug Kauffman, Sung-Il Kim, Jeff Lang, Matt McCrudden, Nancy Risch, Daniel Robinson, Rayne Sperling, and Scott Titsworth. Thank you for challenging me and for sharing the joys of collaboration.

This book was also strengthened by the thorough and thoughtful guidance of reviewers. Many thanks to the reviewers listed below for their insightful comments.

This book could not have been produced were it not for the skilled people that shared in its production. I thank Ken Jensen, Orville Friesen, Mike Jackson, and the Instruction Design Center staff for developing many of the graphics. Thanks as well to Cindy DeRyke for word processing assistance. I also thank the Corwin Press production staff that helped spring my ideas to life. Special thanks go to Carol Chambers Collins, Acquisitions Editor, who molded the project with many bright ideas. Thanks also to Brett Ory, Editorial Assistant, Amy Schroller, Production Editor; Codi Bowman, Copy Editor; C&M Digitals, Typesetter; Jeff Bryant, Proofreader; Judy Hunt, Indexer; and Rose Storey, Cover Designer for your diligence and polish.

Most of all, I recognize my family for all they have taught me and done for me along the way. Thanks Frank and Winifred (my parents) for teaching me how to love one's neighbors and family. Thanks, too, Dad for introducing me to exercise and long distance running long before they were fashionable. Thanks, too, Mom for catching me when I rode my tricycle down the basement stairs. I promise to be more careful next time I'm home. Thanks Dard and Diane (my older siblings) for letting me mix with the big kids and for teaching me how to play, get along, and extend curfew. And, I'm sure you had a good reason for telling me that if I accidently flipped the switch at the top of the basement stairs the house would blow up. At least that's what my therapist keeps saying decades later. Thanks Keaton, Anna, and Samuel (my children) for taking me on the ride of my life. Thanks Keaton for letting me tag along and watch expertise unfold as you rose to chess champion. I'm in awe of what you do. Thanks Anna for teaching me the wonders of animals, technology, and music—if that's what you want to call it—and for keeping me laughing. There is definitely a stand-up gig somewhere in your bright future. Thanks Sam for showing an educational psychologist what internal motivation for learning is all about. Thanks, too, for being my tennis, golf, and running partner. I'll try to keep up. Thanks Christine (my wife and fellow teacher) for showing me that all good teaching begins with caring and ends with pride. Thanks, too, for teaching our family to embrace nature as our playmate. Finally, thanks for the untold gifts that flow from your heart. I dedicate this book to you.

Corwin Press gratefully acknowledges the contributions of the following reviewers:

Douglas Bailer
Teacher, High School Science
Earnest Pruett Center of Technology/Walden University
Dutton, AL

Stacy Gardner Dibble
Fifth-Grade Teacher/Reading Coordinator
Prairie Elementary
Worthington, MN

Karen Hall & Lynn Hayes
Elementary Teachers
Oakdale Elementary School
Rock Hill, SC

Ganna Maymind
First-Grade Teacher
Asher Holmes Elementary
Morganville, NJ

Kathy Redford
Teacher
South Gate Middle School
South Gate, CA

Judy Stoehr
Education Consultant
Judy Stoehr Creative Insights
Omaha, NE

About the Author

 Kenneth A. Kiewra is professor of educational psychology at the University of Nebraska–Lincoln. Professor Kiewra is a graduate of the State University of New York at Oneonta and is certified in elementary and secondary English education. Upon graduation, he taught third grade and coached tennis in Miller Place, New York. Dr. Kiewra later earned his PhD from Florida State University and was also on the faculty at Kansas State University and Utah State University. His research pertains to teaching and learning in general and to aspects of the SOAR method in particular. He has authored numerous articles along with two books for students: *Learning to Learn: Making the Transition From Student to Life-Long Learner* and *Learn How to Study and SOAR to Success.* Dr. Kiewra is the former director of the University of Nebraska's Academic Success Center and the former editor of *Educational Psychology Review.* He is a frequent presenter, having made hundreds of presentations to faculty and student groups. For fun, Ken teaches chess to elementary school students, coaches youth soccer, plays golf and tennis, runs, and places orders at Amigos using pseudonyms. Ken and his family especially enjoy riding waves when visiting Long Island and climbing mountains in Colorado. Ken can be contacted at kkiewra1@unl.edu to arrange speaking engagements or to chat about teaching and learning.

PART I

SOAR Strategies

1

Helping Students Soar

In an academic world brimming with caring and skilled educators, we probably all have met one or two teachers who were pedagogically challenged. Consider my fifth-grade teacher, Mr. Bob Rippe. (Of course, I'm not using his real name. His real name was Mr. Robert Rippe. Just kidding.) Mr. Rippe rarely spoke to the class. Instead, he showed a lot of movies—about four or five a day. It seemed like the lights were never on in our classroom. We were known around school as the moles, because we were the kids squinting in the lunchroom and wearing sunglasses on the bus ride home.

Before each movie, Mr. Rippe sent one of the students to the cafeteria to purchase two cartons of milk for him. Kids paid just 10 cents a carton; teachers paid 15, so he saved 5 cents on every carton. This was a significant savings when you have an 8 to 10 carton-a-day habit. Mr. Rippe would chug the milk and then fall asleep at his desk and not stir until the film spun and snapped in the take-up reel. Students meanwhile paid little attention to the movies. Some dozed, others made shadow puppets on the screen, and others snacked on candy and popcorn smuggled in lunchboxes and book bags. After a film, there was no class discussion or reflection, just a short intermission before the next flick. I learned next to nothing from these films. One of the few ideas that stuck came from a film on the planets. I remembered the planet Uranus because, well, it was named Uranus and I was in fifth grade. I suppose Mr. Rippe's cinematic teaching style had some positive carryover; 12 of the 22 students in our class later secured jobs as movie theater projectionists.

MEET TEACHER A WHO HELPS STUDENTS SOAR TO SUCCESS

Coincidently, or through bad planning, the same planet film was shown in sixth grade and I learned light years more. Here is what my sixth-grade teacher, Ms. Rotor, did. (I reversed the order of letters in her name so she could not be identified.) First, she gave students a handout for taking notes as shown in Exhibit 1.1. The handout helped students **select** important ideas from the film. It listed all the planets and beneath each planet name its key characteristics, such as miles from the sun, revolution time, and orbit speed. Space was provided alongside each characteristic for note taking.

Next, she helped us **organize** the planet information by providing a chart for us to complete. It listed the planet names along the top row and the planet characteristics down the left column. We used our completed notes to fill in the cells within the chart. When completed, the chart looked like that in Exhibit 1.2.

Then Ms. Rotor helped us **associate** the planet facts. She stressed learning relationships, not isolated facts. For instance, when studying the chart in Exhibit 1.2 she pointed out that as planets' distance from the sun increases, their revolution time increases and their orbit speed decreases. Inner planets have rocky surfaces and outer planets have slushy surfaces. Inner planets, relative to outer planets, have smaller diameters, fewer moons, and longer rotation times. "Wow," I remember thinking, "Ms. Rotor and a class of sixth graders were finding all these amazing associations that were never mentioned in the film." There was a cosmic order. Ms. Rotor also helped us associate planet facts with our own lives. She pointed out, for example, that we'd be about 44 years old on Mercury but slightly less than a year old on Jupiter.

Last, Ms. Rotor helped us **regulate** our learning by providing us with practice questions like the following. Answering these questions helped us know if we were ready for a real test over this material.

- Which planet is closest to the sun?
- Which planet has the largest diameter?
- What is the relationship between revolution time and orbit speed?
- What is the relationship between diameter and surface?
- On which planet would you be half your age?

Mr. Rippe's and Ms. Rotor's approaches for teaching about the planets—or anything, for that matter—were markedly different. Mr. Rippe guzzled a couple of cartons, tossed the information out there frame by frame, and left us to learn it as best we could. Ms. Rotor helped us learn. She helped us soar to success by helping us **select** important ideas, **organize** and **associate** the ideas, and then **regulate** (SOAR) our learning through practice testing. Ms. Rotor is what I call an "A" teacher: one who teaches so effectively that students cannot help but learn.

EXHIBIT 1.1 Note-Taking Handout to Help Students Select Important Ideas

Planets

Mercury

Miles from the sun: _____

Revolution time: _____

Orbit speed: _____

Diameter: _____

Surface: _____

Moons: _____

Rotation time: _____

Venus

Miles from the sun: _____

Revolution time: _____

Orbit speed: _____

Diameter: _____

Surface: _____

Moons: _____

Rotation time: _____

EXHIBIT 1.2 Completed Organizational Chart

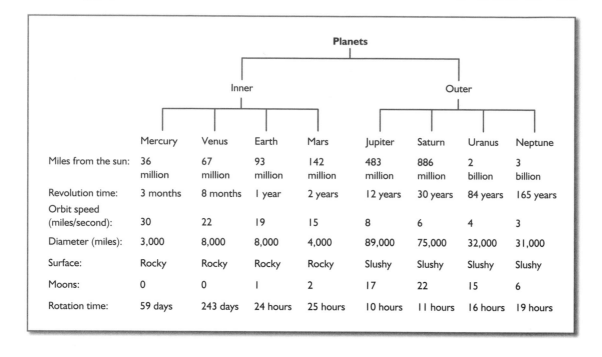

	Mercury	Venus	Earth	Mars	Jupiter	Saturn	Uranus	Neptune
Miles from the sun:	36 million	67 million	93 million	142 million	483 million	886 million	2 billion	3 billion
Revolution time:	3 months	8 months	1 year	2 years	12 years	30 years	84 years	165 years
Orbit speed (miles/second):	30	22	19	15	8	6	4	3
Diameter (miles):	3,000	8,000	8,000	4,000	89,000	75,000	32,000	31,000
Surface:	Rocky	Rocky	Rocky	Rocky	Slushy	Slushy	Slushy	Slushy
Moons:	0	0	1	2	17	22	15	6
Rotation time:	59 days	243 days	24 hours	25 hours	10 hours	11 hours	16 hours	19 hours

The State of Teaching and Learning

Fortunately, most teachers are not as ineffective, sleepy, and lactose tolerant as Mr. Rippe. Unfortunately, most teachers are not as effective as Ms. Rotor. Many do not teach in ways that virtually ensure student learning (Torff & Sessions, 2005; Zimmerman, Bonner, & Kovach, 1996). Many do not teach in ways that help students soar to success. And some go so far as to actually hinder these learning processes. Returning to the planet material, a teacher presenting this material might speak too quickly and make it difficult for students to *select* and note key ideas. The teacher might even discourage or forbid note taking all together, believing that note taking interferes with listening and learning. The teacher might *organize* ideas in an outline (like that shown in Exhibit 1.3) rather than a chart and make it difficult for students to examine ideas across planets—— for instance, their diameters or orbit speeds. The teacher might suggest that students study one planet fact at a time rather than associate ideas and learn relationships. And the teacher might advocate rehearsing planet facts again and again rather than *regulating* learning through self-testing. The teacher doing these things is actually hindering student learning rather than helping it.

What happens when students don't have a teacher that helps them soar, like Ms. Rotor? Can they still learn effectively? They can, and some do, but it's not likely to happen. Students simply presented with the planet information could, on their own, select and note key ideas, organize them, create

EXHIBIT 1.3   Outline Organization That Hinders Association

Planets

Mercury

    Miles from the sun: 36 million

    Revolution time: 3 months

    Orbit speed (miles/second): 30

    Diameter (miles): 3,000

    Surface: rocky

    Moons: 0

    Rotation time: 59 days

Venus

    Miles from the sun: 67 million

    Revolution time: 8 months

    Orbit speed (miles/second): 22

    Diameter (miles): 8,000

    Surface: rocky

    Moons: 0

    Rotation time: 243 days

Earth

    Miles from the sun: 93 million

    Revolution time: 1 year

    Orbit speed (miles/second): 19

    Diameter (miles): 8,000

    Surface: rocky

    Moons: 1

    Rotation time: 24 hours

Mars

    Miles from the sun: 142 million

    Revolution time: 2 years

    Orbit speed (miles/second): 15

    Diameter (miles): 4,000

    Surface: rocky

    Moons: 2

    Rotation time: 25 hours

(Continued)

(Continued)

Jupiter

Miles from the sun: 483 million

Revolution time: 12 years

Orbit speed (miles/second): 8

Diameter (miles): 89,000

Surface: slushy

Moons: 17

Rotation time: 10 hours

Saturn

Miles from the sun: 886 million

Revolution time: 30 years

Orbit speed (miles/second): 6

Diameter (miles): 75,000

Surface: slushy

Moons: 22

Rotation time: 11 hours

Uranus

Miles from the sun: 2 billion

Revolution time: 84 years

Orbit speed (miles/second): 4

Diameter (miles): 32,000

Surface: slushy

Moons: 15

Rotation time: 16 hours

Neptune

Miles from the sun: 3 billion

Revolution time: 165 years

Orbit speed (miles/second): 3

Diameter (miles): 31,000

Surface: slushy

Moons: 6

Rotation time: 19 hours

associations, and regulate learning by self-testing. The problem is that students, left to their devises, rarely soar. Exhibit 1.4 shows what students typically do wrong and what they should do relative to each SOAR component. Instead of selecting all the key ideas and recording them in notes, students usually take sketchy notes while listening (perhaps like those for the first two planets shown in Exhibit 1.5). In fact, students typically record about 35% of important lesson ideas (Kiewra, 1985c). This low level of note taking is damaging because note taking is positively correlated with achievement; the more notes students record, the higher is their achievement (Kiewra & Benton, 1988; Titsworth & Kiewra, 2004). Then, instead of organizing notes in comparative charts, students transform their notes into lists or outlines that obscure relationships among lesson ideas. Students study their notes in a piecemeal fashion, one idea at a time, rather than associating ideas. Moreover, few students regulate learning by self-testing. Instead they study lesson pieces using redundant rehearsal-like strategies such as rereading, reciting, recopying, and regurgitating . . . ridiculous! Rehearsal strategies, although more popular with students than video games, are not effective for remembering information long term.

Want proof? Try now to say the words of the *Star Spangled Banner*—a song you have rehearsed hundreds of times. Or try to recall from memory a prayer you have recited faithfully for years. Not so easy, huh? You are not alone in your struggles. There is a published report about a professor who had read the same four prayers (containing about 500 words) almost daily for 25 years but was unable to recite them from memory. He needed 129 promptings to recite the prayers accurately (Neisser, 1982, p. 177). Although rehearsal is a popular strategy among students preparing for tests (Gubbels, 1999), it is not an effective one (Payne, Klin, Lampinen, Neuschatz, & Lindsay, 1999). To recap, most students are ineffective learners (Gubbels, 1999). Faced with poor instruction, like that of Mr. Rippe, most students lack the strategies necessary to compensate for ineffective instruction and to soar to success.

EXHIBIT 1.4   Ineffective and Effective SOAR Strategies

SOAR Components	Ineffective Strategies	Effective Strategies
Selection	Incomplete note taking	Complete note taking
Organization	Construct linear notes	Construct representations
Association	Piecemeal learning	Build associations
Regulation	Redundant strategies	Self-testing

EXHIBIT 1.5   Sketchy Notes Typical of Student Note Taking

Mercury

    36 million miles

    Speed-30

    3,000 miles

    59 days to rotate

Venus

    8 months around sun

    Speed-22

    Rocky

    243 days

The picture I'm describing is bleak: some teachers just tossing out the material for students to learn or practicing instructional strategies that actually hinder learning and students wielding ineffective strategies like sketchy note taking and rehearsal. How prevalent is ineffective teaching and learning and what are the outcomes?

There are four teaching–learning scenarios that can unfold as shown in Exhibit 1.6. In the first case, instruction is ineffective, students are ineffective learners, and learning is, therefore, minimal. For example, the teacher gives students just an outline of the planet material, and students study it by rehearsing facts. Two negatives do not yield a positive here. With the combination of weak teaching and weak learning skills, students learn little.

EXHIBIT 1.6   Possible Outcomes Resulting From Effective and Ineffective Teaching and Learning

Teaching	Learning	Learning Outcome
Ineffective	Ineffective	Minimal
Effective	Ineffective	Good
Ineffective	Effective	Good
Effective	Effective	Maximal

In the second case, instruction is effective, students are ineffective learners, and learning is good. For example, the teacher provides a framework for selecting and noting key points, a chart for organizing those selected points, a list of important associations, and practice questions to foster regulation. Although students do not know how to apply effective learning strategies on their own, instruction is so good that it compensates for students' weak learning strategies. Good teaching triumphs over weak learning. Students soar to success in spite of their weak learning skills.

In the third case, instruction is ineffective, students are effective learners, and learning is good. For example, the teacher gives students just an outline of the planet material. Students, though, take copious notes, convert the outline to a chart, generate associations, and test themselves over the facts and relationships inherent in the material. Here, learning strategies are so good that they compensate for ineffective teaching. Good learning triumphs over weak instruction. Students soar to success in spite of ineffective instruction.

In the fourth case, instruction is effective, students are effective learners, and learning is maximal. With the best of both worlds—good teaching and good learning—students easily soar to success and beyond.

Knowing that instruction can be effective or ineffective and that students can use effective or ineffective strategies, what is the likelihood of each scenario? No one knows for sure. Reports suggest, however, that instructors often teach in ways that limit learning (Torff & Sessions, 2005) and that most students employ weak and unproductive learning strategies (Gubbels, 1999; Pressley, Yokoi, Van Meter, Van Etten, & Freebern, 1997). Taken together, the teaching–learning system that pervades our schools is broken and needs repair.

Why is the teaching and learning process broken? It is broken, in part, because teachers are not taught to present material in ways that help students soar to success. I surveyed teachers and analyzed the content of educational psychology textbooks and found that prospective teachers were not taught how to design instruction that ensures learning (Kiewra & Gubbels, 1997). It is also broken because many students do not know how to learn, how to soar to success, because they were never instructed in how to learn. It sounds crazy to think that students can spend half their waking hours in school and not be taught to learn, but that is often the case. Teachers teach students content such as math and science, but rarely *how* to learn such content (Durkin, 1979; Zimmerman, Bonner, & Kovach, 1996). Think back through your own educational career. (Stop fixating on the meat-pie medley served in elementary school. Get past that!) You were taught the first amendment to the constitution and how to add mixed fractions, but were you taught how to take a quality set of notes, how to organize those notes, how to create associations, and how to self-test? Were you taught how to manage time or how to foster motivation? Probably not: Schools oddly focus on the products of learning and ignore the processes. Schools focus on what's to be learned but not how to learn it. Consequently, students learn some content but not how to learn.

Why are teachers not teaching students how to learn? One reason is that many educators falsely believe that strategy instruction is remedial. They believe that students develop good learning strategies as naturally as they develop height and weight and therefore good learning habits need not be taught. This logic is flawed. First, if strategies are never taught in the first place, then strategy instruction at any level, by definition, cannot be remedial. Second, strategies do not develop naturally. They are acquired in the same way that musicians acquire talent: through instruction and practice. Without instruction in how to learn, most students pick up weak and sloppy strategies such as sketchy note taking and rehearsal, just as untrained musicians develop weak techniques. I should know. I played guitar unsuccessfully for several years before finally taking a few lessons. It was amazing how rapidly I improved after the instructor offered subtle pointers such as "play the instrument by strumming the strings, not by blowing into it." A second reason that teachers do not teach students how to learn is that many were not taught how to learn when they were students either. Therefore, teachers often advocate the rather weak learning strategies they used as students such as outlining and rehearsing.

MEET TEACHER A+ WHO TEACHES STUDENTS HOW TO SOAR

Since the final destination is student learning, there are two roads toward improving student learning. The first road involves teaching improvement: helping teachers present material so effectively—like Ms. Rotor, like Teacher A—that students learn in spite of their weak strategy repertoire. This road is rather indirect because student learning depends entirely on teacher effectiveness. The student learns fine when instruction is effective but learns little when instruction is poor. The student learns content, like math or science, when it is taught effectively but does not learn how to learn. The second road involves student improvement: helping students acquire effective strategies so they can learn even when instruction is poor. Although this road is more direct and ultimately more beneficial because students hold the keys to learning, it is a rather deserted road. Rarely are students taught how to learn. Two roads, but which is best? Maybe, they are both good. Maybe, they are the same road.

It is possible for teachers to travel both roads simultaneously: Teach effectively so that students soar and teach students *how* to soar. Here is how. First, teachers need to present the material so effectively that students cannot help but learn—just like Ms. Rotor did. This is Teacher A. Recall that Teacher A presents material in ways that enable students to soar to success. Teacher A helps students select key ideas, organize them, create associations, and regulate learning. When this happens, students learn effectively and soar to success.

But effective teaching, like that of Ms. Rotor, only enables students to learn what is effectively taught. It does not enable students to learn when faced with poor instruction, like that of Mr. Rippe. For students to learn under all conditions, they must finally be taught how to learn. But how do teachers teach students how to learn? They do so by teaching effectively—helping students soar—and by simultaneously teaching students how to soar by embedding the teaching of learning strategies in their content teaching.

As teachers teach math, science, history, English, music, physical education, or art, at any level, they have the opportunity, if not the obligation, to also teach students how to learn that content. I call the teacher who teaches strategies Teacher A+. Teacher A+ does the same things as Teacher A—presents material effectively so that students select, organize, associate, and regulate—but while doing so, Teacher A+ also teaches students to do these things on their own. Teacher A helps students soar. Teacher A+ does too but also teaches students *how* to soar.

Embedding strategy instruction is the job of all teachers and one that is easy to carry out. The teaching of learning need not, and should not, occur in a separate class on how to learn. Such adjunct classes often teach learning strategies apart from the students' curriculum. In order for students to learn how to learn, they need practice applying strategies to real coursework. Therefore, strategies are learned best when embedded into content teaching. Embedding strategy instruction involves four simple steps: (a) *introduce* the strategy by modeling and describing it, (b) *sell* the strategy by telling why it works, (c) *generalize* the strategy by telling where else it is helpful, and (d) *perfect* the strategy by providing practice opportunities (Pressley, Woloshyn, & Associates, 1995). As an example, let's revisit Ms. Rotor who provided a chart to help students organize and associate information about planets. While doing this, Ms. Rotor can also teach students how to better organize and associate information as shown in the strategy instruction example below.

"Class, let's take a look at the chart we completed about the planets. This chart strategy is a good one. It groups related information together in a way that you can easily spot associations among the planets. Compare this chart to the planet outline I also provided. Notice that all the information about the planets' orbit speeds is in the same row in the chart but spread across many lines in the outline. With the chart, you can easily glance across the orbit speed row and notice that orbit speed decreases as the planets are positioned further from the sun. This pattern is hard to spot in the outline. Notice, too, how easy it is to see that inner planets are rocky and that outer planets are slushy when looking within a single row of the chart. This same information is only available by reading eight different lines in the outline. So a chart makes it faster and easier for you to spot associations than does an outline." (*Introduce and sell the strategy*)

"Charts are easy to construct. You construct them by putting topics (such as planets) across the top and categories (such as orbit speed and surface features) down the left side. You then put information pertaining to topic and category in the intersecting cell. Let's have you practice by extending this chart to also include the topic Pluto and the category temperature. Your extended chart will reveal why Pluto was exiled. Although it was once considered an outer planet, its odd characteristics were more like those of inner planets. You'll also notice that planet temperature naturally decreases as planets move further from the sun. Let's also think of other science material that is best organized into a chart and practice constructing some of those. I'll begin by constructing a chart about digestion that includes the digestive organs as topics across the top and the categories of location and function down the left side." (*Perfect and generalize the strategy*)

The embedding of strategy instruction is akin to the way that an experienced tradesperson helps an apprentice acquire a trade. As a plumber replaces washers in a faucet or solders pipes, the plumber describes to the apprentice what is being done, how it is being done (*introduce the strategy*), why it is being done (*sell the strategy*), and when and where the plumber might use this technique again (*generalize the strategy*). The tradesperson also provides opportunities for the apprentice to practice (*perfect the strategy*). Through this process, the apprentice learns a skill that is useful now and in future circumstances.

Much is gained by helping students acquire the trade of learning. First, they achieve more in school. They should easily become "A" students. More importantly, they are transformed from restricted learners to autonomous learners capable of learning in any setting. John Bransford (1979, pp. 257–261), a noted psychologist, suggests that restricted learners learn in a slow and gradual manner and that autonomous learners learn in a rapid and exponential manner. The learning curves in Exhibit 1.7 show how restricted and autonomous learners might fare when learning in a single setting, such as a math class, or over their lifetimes. Autonomous learners learn more because they know how to learn whereas restricted learners do not. And because autonomous learners know more, it is easier for them to learn still more because knowledge begets knowledge. The rich indeed get richer.

Another benefit of strategy instruction is that strategic students better control learning and enjoy it more. Too often students dislike learning because they feel out of control, like pawns being pushed around in the game of school. Their instructors, for example, might rapidly toss an endless stream of unrelated facts at them, and then test students without revealing how they will be tested. Consequently, students feel frustrated and lost. Students overwhelmed with unorganized information and given

EXHIBIT 1.7   Learning Curve for Restricted and Autonomous Learners

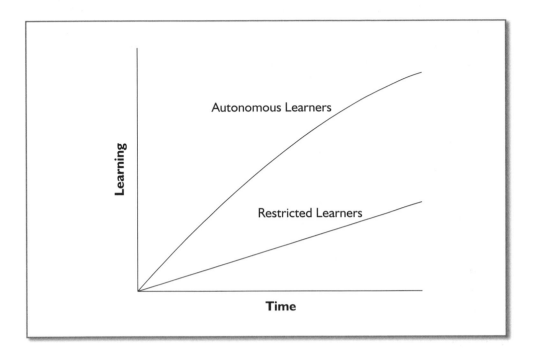

no test knowledge, though, can create order among this disorder and control their learning by using effective strategies. Students can take copious notes, organize them, create associations, and regulate learning through self-testing. If an effective instructor can facilitate learning, then strategic students can too.

Students might also believe they lack control because the instructor speaks in a way that is hard to hear or is boring. But even in these situations, simple strategies put students in control. Students can usually move forward to better hear a quiet instructor or ask the instructor to repeat what was not heard. I'll never forget attending a national conference and listening to a prominent speaker addressing 1,000 people in a crowded room. The speaker kept moving away from the microphone making it difficult to hear him. Finally, one woman in the last row stood up on her chair and screamed, "Will you please use the microphone!?" That's taking control. Returning to the instructor-is-boring problem—not a problem. Taking a detailed set of notes is incompatible with boredom. When students take a high quality set of notes, they control boredom.

Let me sum up and speak a bit about fishing. In education, we need instructors like Teacher A who teach in ways that help students soar. But we need more. Recall the old adage, if you give a man a fish, you feed him for a day, but if you teach him how to fish, he'll drink a lot of beer and get sunburned. No, that's not it; if you teach him how to fish, you feed him for a lifetime. Instructor A, who helps students soar, is a good "fish giver." Students receive the means to learn what is being taught right now. What more can Instructor A do? Be a good fishing teacher. Be Teacher A+. As you teach in ways that help students soar, teach them how to soar. Embed the teaching of learning strategies in content instruction so that the fishing pole is gradually transferred from your hands to students' hands, thereby helping them learn now and for a lifetime.

WHERE WE GO FROM HERE

The goal of this text, then, is to improve instruction so that teachers help students soar and teach them how to soar. Consequently, each of the next four chapters in Part I pertains to one of the SOAR strategies, respectively—select, organize, associate, and regulate. Each chapter describes what teachers should do to foster learning and teach students how to learn. In Part II, I present additional chapters on motivation and classroom management because students need these support strategies to soar. Finally, the text concludes with a supporting chapter on how to help students soar to the heights of extraordinary talent.

2

Helping Students Select

Chapter 2 is about the first step in the SOAR process: *selecting* important information. Recall from Chapter 1 that students must *select* important information, *organize* and *associate* that information, and then *regulate* learning through self-testing. Without selection, students are grounded from the start and cannot soar. The first part of Chapter 2 mentions four classroom issues likely to sabotage information selection. These are poorly structured environments, inefficient routines, lack of teacher with-it-ness, and task overload. All these situations share a common feature: They divert attention away from what students should select. Next, we'll see just how attention works and how teachers can control it. The last part of Chapter 2 examines five instructional methods that help students select and note important lesson information: complete notes, skeletal notes, lesson cues, re-presentation, and reconstruction.

CLASSROOM ISSUES LIKELY TO SABOTAGE INFORMATION SELECTION

As a newly hired third-grade teacher, I was wonderfully organized—or so I thought. One day, I listed four assignments on the board for students to complete at their seats. I explained each assignment in turn and at length. I then placed four baskets on my desk at the front of the room, one for each assignment, and directed students to bring each to my desk as it was completed. While students worked through these assignments, I summoned small groups of students to the back of the room to work with me on their reading skills. All the while, a jazz recording played while students worked. I had read somewhere that musical intelligence is fostered by playing background music. My planning would yield a quiet and distraction-free environment for students and me to work. Wrong!

Students summoned to work with me on reading skills rifled through their desks, searching for reading materials. Books crashed to the floor and papers flew. With cradled books, papers, and pencils finally in hand, students dragged their chairs through a maze of student desks. Chair and desk legs clanged and bumped like race cars jockeying for position. Books and papers were knocked to the ground. Students argued like lawyers over who was at fault. When the students finally arrived, they positioned their chairs along the back wall; I faced them and turned my back on the other students completing seatwork. Consequently, I never saw the seatwork students copy one another's answers, daydream, or play air saxophone along with the jazz recording. What I did see was an unbroken line of students at my side seeking assignment clarification. "What is it we're supposed to do again in Assignment 1 (or 2, 3, and 4)?" they asked, having forgotten or confused assignment directions.

Meanwhile, as students completed each of the four assignments, they dutifully and successively brought each one to my desk. Do the math. Twenty-five students each turning in four assignments meant that students were out of their seats 100 times just turning in assignments. And no third-grade student takes a direct and purposeful route to a teacher's desk. Instead, students wound circuitously about the classroom pausing occasionally to chat with friends, grind their pencils into nubs at the sharpener, and slurp long drinks at the water fountain. You get the picture. My classroom had more traffic and more ups and downs than O'Hare Airport. In my attempt to create a distraction-free environment, I created a monster. With all the noise and commotion, students and I had trouble selecting the information needed to do our work.

This scenario showcases four classroom issues that sabotage information selection. First, my classroom was a *poorly structured environment.* I could better structure the environment as shown in Exhibit 2.1. The restructured classroom has a reading center in the room's back corner. Student groups meeting with me for reading now have a quiet out-of-the-way place to work so that neither they nor students working at their desks are disturbed. The reading center has a comfortable rug, couches, and a table and chairs. Students summoned to the reading center no longer need to drag their chairs with them.

Second, I used *inefficient routines.* Rather than have students hand in each of four assignments as they finish it, students can hold all their work and pass it in at the end of class. If I needed to check Assignment 2 right away, I could do so by circulating from desk to desk or by asking all students to pause and pass in that assignment. Either way, the parade of students moving about the classroom is canceled. As for the problem of

EXHIBIT 2.1   Improved Classroom Arrangement to Deter Distractions

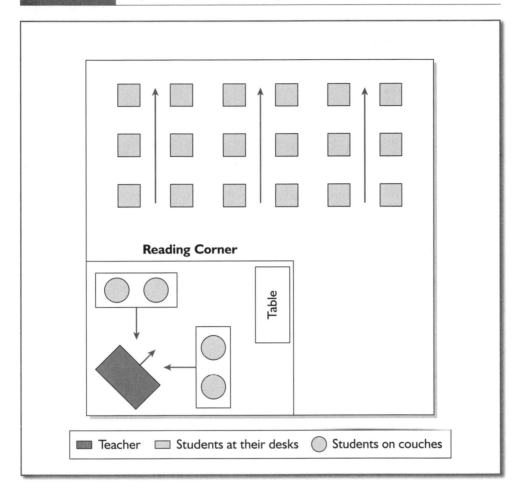

students rifling through their desks searching for their reading materials and distracting others quietly working, I can simply ask all students to place their reading materials on their desk at the start of class.

Third, I *lacked with-it-ness* (Kounin, 1970). With-it teachers are aware of what is going on throughout the classroom. They seemingly have eyes in the back of their heads. And that's exactly what I needed when I naively turned my back on students completing seatwork. Doing so made it hard for me to monitor them and hard for them to get my attention. In the improved classroom setting shown in Exhibit 2.1, I face the reading group and the seat workers so that I can monitor all students. Moreover, the reading group faces away from the other students, so neither group is distracted.

Last, I created *task overload* by issuing four assignments at once and by playing jazz music. Students were overwhelmed trying to remember directions for four assignments. I should have explained assignments one at a time or given students written instructions they could reference before beginning a new assignment. The jazz music also overloaded attention. When the beat quickened or trumpets blared, students paused from their work to listen.

There is a common theme among these classroom issues: Students' attention is diverted from information that should be selected to other information. While students' attention should be focused on assignment completion or reading skills, it is instead diverted to crashing books, flying papers, clanging chairs, slurping water, and the like. You might believe that students need to just buckle down and pay attention to their work. Unfortunately, human brains do not operate that way. Brains make attention diversion more the rule than the exception. Teachers must, therefore, engineer environments and establish routines that promote rather than hinder attention. Moreover, they must be with-it and minimize task overload to keep students attentive.

HOW ATTENTION WORKS AND HOW TEACHERS CAN CONTROL IT

To further understand how the brain works and how teachers can foster attention, we must review the methods and findings from a classic study of attention (Cherry, 1953). Although this study was conducted in a laboratory, I describe how I conduct it as a classroom demonstration in case you decide to replicate it with your students. It is called the shadowing demonstration. I ask one student to stand and read from the university newspaper. (All students have a copy that they enjoy reading during class.) A second student stands facing the first and repeats (shadows) every word that is read. As if shadowing isn't demanding enough, I stand behind the shadower and deliver a second or unshadowed message. I intermittently read from a textbook, recite nursery rhymes, speak in German, raise and lower my voice, whistle, bang on the table, cough, flick the lights, gesture for students in the class to stand and sit back down, say a designated word prearranged with the shadower (such as *pizza*), and call the shadower by name. I then ask the shadower about the experience. Shadowers report that shadowing is difficult, comprehension of the shadowed message is close to zero, and there is only mild awareness of other things happening in the room. When pressed on this last issue, shadowers report that they heard me read but did not even know the topic. They report not hearing the change in language or the stuff I said about their family.

Four Types of Stimuli That Capture Attention

It is informative to note what shadowers capture from the unshadowed message. They detect *novel stimuli*, such as whistling, banging, coughing, increased voice volume, and flickering lights. They detect *movement*, such as when individuals in the class stand up. They detect things that are *familiar*, such as a nursery rhyme and their name. And they detect things they are *searching for*, such as the predetermined word (*pizza*). These four types of things grabbed the shadower's attention.

How can teachers use the information stemming from the shadowing demonstration? In two ways: one, to channel students' attention toward what they should select and, two, to limit distractions that divert attention. For example, if we know that students pay attention to things they are looking for, then we can tell them what to look for during instruction. If we know that movement commands attention, then we can limit movement that might commandeer attention. Let's see how each type of attention grabber might guide or misguide attention in the classroom.

Novel or unusual stimuli grab attention. We tend to notice the yellow rose among the red ones or the one house in the neighborhood that stands out because of its odd design or color. Teachers can take advantage of this tendency by presenting information in novel ways that command attention. One simple way to do this is by varying voice. Occasionally speaking louder, softer, faster, slower, higher, lower, or more emphatically are ways to command attention. Similarly, when writing on the board or preparing PowerPoint slides, a teacher can use novel attention getters by changing font color, size, and style. Words can also be bolded, italicized, underlined, enlarged, or minimized to grab attention. Teachers must be cautious not to present a novel stimulus so often that it loses its novelty—much like the boy who repeatedly cried wolf. An occasional bang on the desk directs attention. Repeated banging produces habituation and no rise in attention. Similarly, screaming, "Be quiet! I've had it with you," might work a few times, but it probably draws little attention once students habituate to the screaming complaint.

Novel teaching methods also command attention. A government and law instructor taught students about the legal system by showing video clips from actual trials and having students play legal roles in a mock trial. A history teacher reviewed course content by simulating the game *Who Wants to Be a Millionaire*. And an English teacher began grammar lessons by citing grammar bloopers from popular culture.

Novelty can distract as well. Television commercials strive for novelty to command attention, but sometimes that novelty obscures the intended message. I remember a commercial where people topple over like dominoes. It was certainly original, but I cannot recall the product. In the classroom, unintended novelty can pull students off task. A peeping classroom pet, an unerased chalkboard cluttered with definitions and diagrams from yesterday's lessons, and the aroma of pizza baking in the cafeteria can all derail attention. One of the classrooms I teach in is oddly situated beneath a gymnastics facility. The sounds of tumbles and dismounts sometimes echo in our classroom and pull students (and me) off task.

Movement commands attention. A flying insect or crawling bug spotted out of the corner of your eye draws your attention away from most any task. Have you wondered why you've witnessed so many falling stars in your lifetime? It's because your eyes detect movement better than a motion detector. This ability probably stems from our ancestral days when detecting movement in the periphery kept humans from being lion chow.

Instructors can command attention by moving about the room or using hand gestures. When students are distracted or off task, moving close to them regains attention. Be careful, though, because moving stimuli can also distract students. An instructor who repeatedly waves his arms might draw attention away from the intended message to his flailing arms. Teachers should also try to keep student movement to a minimum. We have already seen that a poorly conceived paper-turning-in routine can produce excessive and unnecessary movement. Even minor movement can distract. I remember sitting in a class where the student in front of me continually swung his leg back and forth like a metronome. There was no ignoring this movement. To escape it, I gradually turned in my seat until I nearly faced the back wall.

Familiar stimuli grab attention too. Suppose that you are speaking to someone in a crowded room—perhaps at a party or in a cafeteria—where dozens of other conversations are occurring. Much like the shadowing demonstration, you are aware that others are conversing, but you do not know what they are saying. Then, someone casually mentions the name of your hometown or your mother's name and your ears perk up. Your attention shifts from your own conversation to that where the familiar information was spoken. Familiar visual information is just as luring. I remember attending a basketball game at Kansas State University. During this particular game, several large get well cards for our recovering coach were passed around for signing. When a card with perhaps 75 signatures reached me, I quickly signed it and began passing it along. As I passed it, I noticed a familiar name that seemed to jump off the list. I would have sworn that I did not look at a single name on the list, and yet that familiar name caught my attention.

Instructors can command attention by using examples familiar to students. In the past, familiar names from Tony the Tiger to Tiger Woods have been excellent attention getters. Teachers might be more successful teaching the possessive case when the umbrella belongs not to Professor Smith but to Professor Dumbledore. Children learning about supply and demand might attend better to a familiar example about gasoline prices than a less familiar example about soybeans.

Things that we are looking for also capture attention. There is an old adage, "When a thief meets a saint, all he sees are his pockets." People notice what they are looking for, often to the exclusion of other things. Dentists notice teeth, not hands; mechanics notice fuel pumps, not car mats. I once looked for a friend among thousands of people in the starting area of the New York City Marathon. After surveying the masses for a few seconds, I spotted him. Humans have an uncanny knack for finding the needle in the haystack when looking for it. It is car keys we can never find!

Teachers can prime students to seek out particular stimuli. Providing students with signals such as prequestions or preobjectives alerts them to attend to particular information. But there is a cost. Exhibit 2.2 compares the hypothetical test performance of students who receive prequestions or preobjectives and those who are unaided. The left portion of Exhibit 2.2 shows that students receiving the instructional aids outperform those without aids on test questions pertaining to the prequestions or preobjectives. This is called intentional learning because the instructional aids were intended to focus attention on this material. The right portion of Exhibit 2.2, however, shows that students receiving the instructional aids perform worse than students without aids on test questions not directly pertaining to the prequestions or preobjectives. This is called incidental learning because the instructional aids did not focus on this material. Overall, these results confirm that instructional aids presented prior to instruction, such as prequestions and preobjectives, focus attention on material signaled by

| **EXHIBIT 2.2** | Intentional and Incidental Performance for Students With and Without Instructional Aids |

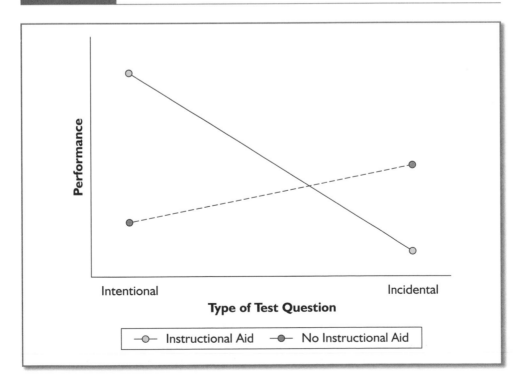

the aids but detract attention away from material not signaled by the aids (Anderson & Biddle, 1975; Boker, 1974). Therefore, teachers should use prequestions or preobjectives that signal all the information they want students to select and learn.

Two Types of Attention: Automatic and Selective

Psychologists purport, and the shadowing demonstration suggests, that there are two levels of attention: automatic and selective. When shadowing, selective attention is allocated to the message being shadowed, and automatic attention is allocated to all other stimuli that enter in through the five senses. Some of the stimuli processed automatically, however, are salient enough to command selective attention. In which case, selective attention shifts, at least temporarily, from the shadowed message to a bang, movement, or word, for example, stemming from the nonshadowed message.

Here is another example of the interplay between automatic and selective attention. As you walk through a crowded corridor at school you might notice a student you had been meaning to speak with, a poster announcing a fund-raiser for diabetes research, and a girl with blue spiked hair. All of these stimuli were attended to selectively. But how and why were these things selected for attention? Actually, as you walked the corridor, all stimuli from the environment entered briefly into what is called sensory memory where they are automatically held and scanned so that you can determine which merit further selective attention. As you walk down the hall, then, you automatically attend to not only the student you were looking for but to all students, not only to the diabetes fund-raising poster (a familiar cause you staunchly support) but to all posters tacked to the wall, and not only to novel blue spiked hair but to all styles of hair. Automatically, without conscious awareness, you hold and scan all available stimuli looking for ones worthy of increased attention. Once found, you attend selectively to those stimuli. Coming at it from another angle, it is automatic attention that keeps you from bumping into other people or from falling down stairs as you walk through school. But automatic attention alone cannot reveal what those people look like or the pattern of tile on the stairs. It is only when you apply selective attention that you focus on a stimulus and fully grasp its properties or message.

The interplay between automatic and selective attention holds important implications for teaching and learning. In particular, it addresses the practical question: How many things can students pay attention to simultaneously? You might believe that students have the capacity to pay attention to multiple tasks. After all, we are a multitasking society. We converse on our cell phones as we drive. We surf the Internet or check e-mail while watching television. American youth are the wizards of electronic multitasking. They are plugged into some electronic media an astounding six and a half hours a day but actually pack eight and half hours of exposure into that time (see Wallis, 2006) as they juggle music, Web surfing, instant messaging, television, and Toaster Strudels.

With students' apparent ability to multitask, should teachers load up on instruction? Should they present new material on the area of triangles while students complete review problems on the area of rectangles? Should they show a video on fulcrums while students surf the Internet looking for examples of fulcrums? Absolutely not!

The human brain does not multitask. It is a serial processor that can focus on just one thing at a time. It is incapable of devoting selective attention to multiple things. It is either the Internet or television. There is no simultaneous processing. Instead we toggle rapidly from stimulus to stimulus, changing channels faster than a couch potato with an infrared remote. Because we are serial processors—even fast ones—research confirms that when people multitask, they make more errors and actually use more time than if the tasks were carried out separately (Strayer, Drews, & Johnston, 2003; also see Wallis, 2006). The obvious implication is that teachers should not overload students' attention resources. Students can allocate attention to just one thing at a time. Students cannot copy a diagram from the board and listen intently to a lesson. The limits of selective attention demand that they do one or the other at any given time.

If humans can focus on only one stimulus at a time, then how do we fold laundry while watching television, converse while driving a car, and record notes while listening to a lesson? The reason is automaticity. Certain well-practiced tasks become automatic, meaning that selective attention is no longer necessary for carrying them out. Folding laundry, taking notes, and, yes, even driving a car are well-practiced tasks that you can do without really thinking about them. When you do something automatically, selective attention can be allocated elsewhere such as to television viewing, conversing, or reading. It takes a lot of practice to develop automaticity and, sometimes, selective attention is still needed to carry out what is typically an automatic task. Consider driving. When you drive, you do other things such as tune the radio, converse with a passenger, consult a map, and paint your toenails. Driving is a skill done automatically. But it wasn't always this way. When you first got behind the wheel, all your selective attention was focused on driving. You thought about shifting, breaking, regulating speed, and many other driving tasks. Only with practice did driving become automatic. And driving is still not always automatic. Sometimes you must downshift to selective attention. Even after years of experience, driving in unfamiliar territory in a nighttime fog or snowstorm requires all your selective attention and then some. Your attention is riveted on driving, and the radio program you were listening to earlier fades to the background.

The notion of automaticity has important instructional implications. It suggests that attention can be divided only when a particular task is made automatic through practice. New and poor readers, for example, have trouble comprehending a story because much of their attention is spent trying to decode words. Good readers, meanwhile, have acquired effective decoding and word recognition skills so that these basic tasks are carried out automatically while selective attention is used for the more demanding task of comprehension. The Florida State football team once lost a game because an automatic task suddenly required selective attention. The team's first- and second-string centers were injured requiring an unpracticed replacement to fill in at the last minute. Florida State fumbled three center exchanges in the first half alone and mishandled others. Needless to say, their offense sputtered. The poor center snaps did more than cause problems advancing the football. The quarterback was suddenly attending to rudimentary center snaps rather than defensive alignments and game strategy. A typically automatic task had gone selective and sacked the quarterback's attention to leadership duties.

It is amazing what can happen when we automate certain skills. I have read that individuals can take flawless dictation and read a novel with comprehension when the task of taking dictation is well practiced and automatic. Master chess players can make all their moves for an entire game in one minute or less because they rapidly recognize familiar chess patterns and react to them automatically. Experts in any field, whether it is bricklaying, baking, tennis, music, or medicine, are able to do with one stroke of attention what most of us would be able to do only with six or seven strokes. The implications are clear. Certain basic tasks such as reading, mastering math facts, gripping a golf club, and keyboarding should be mastered and made automatic in order to free selective attention for more cognitively demanding tasks.

SELECTING AND NOTING
THE INTENDED MESSAGE

When I was a graduate student at Florida State University, I took a statistics course from Professor Harold Fletcher. Dr. Fletcher forbade note taking. He reasoned that if students are busy jotting notes, then they are not carefully listening to and thinking about the material. Dr. Fletcher gave students a complete set of notes following each lesson so they had a record of the lesson and material to study. Most students were delighted with this arrangement. They could sit back and enjoy the lesson, not worry about note taking, and still have a set of notes to review. I was not among the delighted. I was a voracious note taker who often filled up pages with notes while others recorded just a few lines. I found my standard notes to be more detailed than Dr. Fletcher's and therefore better for studying. Moreover, I felt that note taking helped me pay attention during a lecture rather than distract me.

Because I could not overtly record notes in Dr. Fletcher's class, I became a closet note taker. I sat in the back of the room shielded behind a former offensive lineman who had let himself go. I quickly jotted notes when Professor Fletcher turned to write on the board or looked away. Sometimes I resorted to trickery. I'd pretend that I was ill and cradle my head in my arms on the desk forming a small, dark alcove for note taking. Or, I'd give a glance and a quick wave toward the door as if someone was there. When Dr. Fletcher looked that way, I scribbled feverishly. Outright lying was called for on occasion. One time, Dr. Fletcher crept surreptitiously to the back of the room while I sat huddled over a tiny notepad recording a statistical formula. "Mr. Kiewra," he bellowed now standing over me, "are you recording notes in my class?" "Ah, no," I fibbed, "I'm, ah, writing a letter to a friend back home." Dr. Fletcher grinned and replied, "Oh, thank goodness. I thought you were recording notes."

Note taking (like I was doing) and note having (like Professor Fletcher arranged) both boost achievement (Kiewra, 1985a). The process of taking notes focuses students' attention on instruction and prevents daydreaming or other activities like reading the newspaper or checking cell phone messages. That's why it's better for students to record notes during a lesson than simply listen. Having notes—whether provided or self-generated—is also helpful because notes provide a permanent record of ideas in a location outside our sometimes feeble and fading memory that are available later for review. That's why it is better for students to review notes than not review.

In most classrooms from middle schools on up, students commonly take notes; they just don't take enough of them. Ninety-nine percent of college students, for example, record notes (Palmatier & Bennet, 1974), yet note taking is incomplete. On average, students record just 35% of important lesson ideas (Kiewra, 1985c) even though note taking is positively correlated with achievement (Kiewra & Benton, 1988). The more notes students record, the higher their achievement. More specifically, students have about a 50% chance of recalling noted information on a test but only about a 5% chance of recalling non-noted information (Bretzing & Kulhavy, 1981; Howe, 1970).

Students' tendency to scrimp on note taking might be the result of ignorance—not realizing that more note taking is associated with higher achievement—or effort. It is hard, hand-cramping work recording a complete set of notes. In fact, students record fewer notes in the second half of lessons when fatigued than in the first half (Locke, 1977). Teachers, too, might be at the root of limited note taking. Dr. Fletcher, as you just read, outlawed note taking in the classroom. Teachers can also inhibit note taking by speaking too rapidly. At higher speaking rates, students record fewer notes than at lower speaking rates (Ladas, 1980). Thankfully, there are things teachers can do to boost student note taking or note having. A description of those note-facilitating techniques follows.

Before dismissing these techniques, thinking that your students are too young to benefit from note taking, think again. If students can read and write, they can benefit from note taking or note having. The techniques presented here are either geared toward aiding note taking or providing notes for review. Moreover, several of the techniques direct attention to information that should be selected even if notes are not recorded.

Provide Complete Notes

One obvious strategy for increasing the quantity of notes available to students is for instructors to provide a complete set of notes to review, as Professor Fletcher did for his statistics students. Research shows that students who listen to a lesson and later review instructor-provided notes actually outperform students who record and review their own notes. This is because the instructor's notes are usually far more complete than students' notes (Kiewra, 1985c).

One study (Kiewra, 1985b) went so far as to show that reviewing the instructor's notes is so effective, it can compensate for missing the lesson. Exhibit 2.3 shows the achievement for several groups that differed in their acquisition and review conditions. At acquisition, students listened to the lesson without recording notes, listened and recorded notes, or absented themselves from the lesson. At review, students studied their own notes, the instructor's notes, both sets of notes, or no notes. As seen in the right column of Exhibit 2.3, those reviewing the instructor's notes achieved the most. Those without notes to review achieved the least. And those who reviewed their own notes achieved in the midrange. The notes were also

EXHIBIT 2.3   The Benefits of Reviewing the Instructor's Notes

Groups	Test Performance
Take notes/review own plus instructor's notes	71%
Not attend/review instructor's notes	69%
Listen/review instructor's notes	63%
Take notes/review own notes	51%
Take notes/review no notes	44%
Listen/review no notes	43%
Not attend/review no notes	33%
All participants	53%

analyzed. Students recording their own notes only wrote down about 35% of the important lesson ideas. The instructor's notes, meanwhile, contained all the important ideas.

These findings confirm that it is important to have a complete set of notes to review. Regardless of what students did at acquisition—listen, record notes, or absent themselves—their learning hinged on the completeness of the notes reviewed. The implication is that because student note taking is so incomplete, instructors can aid student learning by providing students with complete notes to study. This implication might be especially vital in elementary grades where note taking is minimal or nonexistent. Of course, many instructors are too busy to generate complete notes or simply believe that note taking is the students' responsibility. For those instructors, there is perhaps a middle ground: providing skeletal notes.

Provide Skeletal Notes

Skeletal notes get their name because they are akin to the bones of a skeleton. Skeletal notes contain the lesson's main ideas (bones) interspersed with spaces for students to jot more detailed notes about those main ideas. The notes recorded are like flesh on the skeletal bones. In a study investigating skeletal notes (Kiewra, Benton, Kim, Risch, & Christensen, 1995), researchers directed students who attended a lesson on the topic of creativity to record notes on their own or on the skeletal framework shown in Exhibit 2.4. Those taking their own notes recorded 38% of the important lesson ideas. Skeletal note takers recorded 56% of the important lesson ideas. This boost in note taking produced a comparable boost in achievement when students were tested over the lesson. Instructors providing skeletal notes should be sure to provide ample space for note taking. Research confirms that student note taking increases as the size of the note-taking space increases (Hartley, 1976).

Provide Lesson Cues

Another instructional strategy for increasing note taking is providing lesson cues. Two types of cues boost note taking: importance cues and organizational cues. Cues signaling importance can be written on the chalkboard or projected onto a screen, presented orally, or delivered nonverbally. In one study investigating lesson cues (Locke, 1977), students recorded 86% of information written on the chalkboard—a huge increase from the roughly 35% of lesson points students normally record without cueing. Students are so adept at jotting notes from the chalkboard that I have noticed many students copying the scribbles left behind by the classroom's previous instructor, who forgot to erase the board.

EXHIBIT 2.4   Skeletal Notes for a Lesson on Creativity

Creativity

Expressive Creativity

Definition:

Time demand:

Motivation:

Characteristics:

Myths:

Adaptive Creativity

Definition:

Time demand:

Motivation:

Characteristics:

Myths:

There are many ways to signal importance. An instructor can say that a point is "noteworthy," "imperative," "more important than air," or as one of my college professors used to say, "absolutely critical." The not-too-subtle phrase, "This will be on the test," also works to raise note taking. Sometimes it is not what you say but how you say it that signals importance. Variance in voice pitch, cadence, volume, or rate can let students know that information is noteworthy. Repeating a word or phrase is also a sure sign of importance (or early onset of memory dysfunction).

One college instructor I had emphasized important points nonverbally by cradling his chin in his hand, jutting out his bottom lip, arching his eyebrows, and nodding his head vehemently. His students were alert for this cue and wrote feverishly when they saw it. In a reported research study (Moore, 1968), a lecturer held up cards signaling whether information should be noted or not noted. When a green card was held up students knew to take notes. When a red card was held aloft, students knew to stop taking notes. Other nonverbal signals of importance might include pointing, clapping, finger snapping, hand waving, a piercing glance, or a knock on a table. Saying nothing is also a cue. When instructors pause after making an important point, students recognize this as a signal for note taking.

Organizational cues are those that alert students to the organization of the lesson. When these cues are delivered during instruction, they raise note taking and achievement. In a study investigating organizational lesson cues (Titsworth & Kiewra, 2004), college students listened to one of two versions of a lesson about communication theories: cued and uncued. Both versions were well organized and identical with one exception: The cued lesson signaled the lesson's organization by emphasizing the four lesson topics (the names of the communication theories) and five lesson categories common to each topic (e.g., definition, example, application). For instance, one cue was, "Next we examine an *application* of *general systems theory.*" Another was, "Here is the *definition* of *mass media theory.*" There were 20 organizational cues in total. After the lesson, there was a brief review period followed by two tests. The organization test measured knowledge of the lesson's structure. The detail test measured knowledge of the lesson details at the intersection of lesson topics and categories. The notes were also analyzed for organizational points and details.

Cues impacted note taking and achievement. Exhibit 2.5 shows the number of organizational points and details recorded in notes for those hearing the cued and uncued lessons. Students receiving organizational cues recorded more organizational points and details than students not receiving cues. Most telling was the percentage of noted details. Uncued students noted just 37% of the lesson's details, whereas cued students noted 80% of the details—an astounding increase. In terms of achievement, Exhibit 2.6 shows much higher achievement for the cued students than for the uncued students on both the organization and detail tests. Cuing raised achievement about sevenfold and twofold on the organization and detail tests, respectively. Overall, this study confirms that signaling a lesson's organization boosts note taking and achievement. Such cues are effective and easy to deliver.

EXHIBIT 2.5   Percentage of Notes Recorded During Cued and Uncued Lessons

	Notes	
	Organization Points	Detail Points
Lecture		
Cues	54	80
No cues	15	37

EXHIBIT 2.6	Percentage Correct on Organization and Detail Tests for Groups With and Without Organizational Lecture Cues

	Tests	
	Organization	*Detail*
Groups		
Cues	53	37
No cues	8	21

Re-Present the Lesson

Another strategy for increasing note taking is re-presenting the lesson. In a research study (Kiewra, Mayer, Christensen, Kim, & Risch, 1991), college students recorded notes while watching a brief videotaped lesson presented one, two, or three times. Students in a fourth group watched individually and controlled video play. They could pause, rewind, and replay the lesson or any portion of it. The graph in Exhibit 2.7 shows the percentage of main ideas and supporting details that students recorded. Looking at the striped lines representing main ideas, it is apparent that students adequately recorded the most important ideas even viewing the lesson just one time. All groups recorded about 80% of the main ideas. Although groups were equally effective noting main ideas, they differed in noting lesson details. Looking at the shaded lines representing details, it is evident that students viewing the video lesson twice (53%), three times (60%), or on their own (65%) recorded more details than students viewing the video lesson just once (38%). The note-taking results were mirrored in test results. Groups that recorded more detailed notes outperformed those with less detailed notes.

It is obviously unrealistic to expect teachers to repeat their lessons. In this day of advanced technology, however, it is often possible, and even simple, to make lessons available on video and audio recorders or on computers where students can access them and replay them. When students replay a lesson, they record more detailed notes and raise achievement beyond what's gained from one presentation of the lesson.

Reconstruct Lesson Notes

A fifth strategy for increasing note taking called *reconstruction* actually occurs following the lesson. Students are encouraged to review their notes in hopes that their recorded notes prompt them to reconstruct and add missing lesson points. For example, suppose that students heard the brief

EXHIBIT 2.7	Percentage of Main Ideas and Details Noted for One, Two, Three Presentations of the Lesson, and for Free Viewing

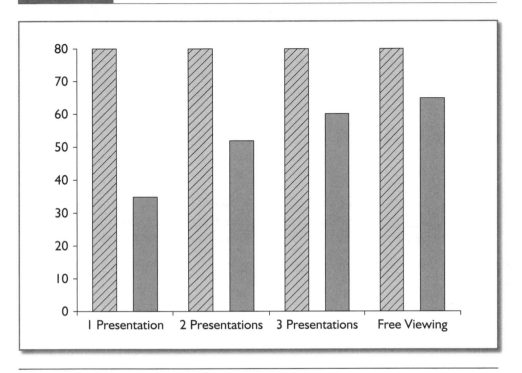

NOTE: Striped lines represent main ideas recorded in notes; shaded lines represent details recorded in notes.

lesson about young marriages shown in Exhibit 2.8. The left portion of Exhibit 2.9 shows a typical set of incomplete notes that a student might record. If the student reviews these notes soon after the lesson while memory is fresh, the student can use those existing notes as cues for reconstructing lesson points absent from notes. The right portion of Exhibit 2.9 shows the student's postlesson reconstructions.

Several informal studies I have conducted with my classes show that reconstruction commonly boosts note completeness from about 35% to about 50%. Students reconstructing notes with a partner boost the number of noted lesson points even higher. This greater increase is probably because of a combination of note sharing (noting a point your partner had that you did not have) and collaborative reconstruction. Whatever the reason, students' individual or joint attempts to embellish notes following the lesson seem worthwhile.

In summary, instructors working with students at almost any level can help them select key ideas and boost note completeness by providing (a) a complete set of notes, (b) skeletal notes, (c) lesson cues, (d) copies of the lesson for re-presentation, or (e) opportunities to reconstruct missed points soon after the lesson. These instructional strategies, although immediately

EXHIBIT 2.8   Brief Lesson About Young Marriage

Young Marriage

The marriages with the poorest track record for success are those in which each partner is below the age of 18. Also, when both partners are school dropouts, there is little chance of success. When the female is pregnant prior to marriage, the prognosis for the marriage is also grim.

Marriages with an intermediate chance of success are characterized by females being age 17 or older and males being age 20 or older. The female has dropped out of high school but the male has graduated from high school. The couple does not begin marriage with a pregnancy but conceives a child immediately after the marriage.

Marriages with the best chance of success are those in which the partners are high school graduates. Pregnancy does not occur until at least one year after the marriage. The partners are older. The female is at least 18 and the male is at least 20.

EXHIBIT 2.9   Incomplete Notes Plus Reconstructions

Incomplete Notes   *Reconstructions*

Young Marriage

Poor ------------------------------- chance for success
    Below age 18 ------------------- both partners
    Dropouts ----------------------- from high school
    Pregnant before ---------------- marriage

Intermediate --------------------- chance for success
    Female 17 --------------------- or older, male 20+
    Male graduates ---------------- from high school
    Pregnant after ---------------- marriage

Best Chance
    High school ------------------- both graduate high school
    Pregnant after ---------------- 1 year
    Older ------------------------- female 18+, male 20+

helpful, do not necessarily empower students to do these things on their own in future settings. As was discussed in Chapter 1, students need strategy instruction in order to acquire and apply strategies.

STRATEGY INSTRUCTION: TEACHING STUDENTS TO SELECT

The narrative below is an example of how an instructor teaching European History might promote note taking and simultaneously teach a note-taking strategy. Notice that the four components of strategy instruction introduced in Chapter 1 are apparent.

> "Class, I noticed that many of you recorded incomplete notes when I spoke last week about the French Revolution. Here is a set of complete notes that I created from that lesson to model good note taking. I numbered each lesson point that I recorded, and you can see there were 90 key points. Quickly examine your notes from that lesson and count how many of those points you have." (*Introduce the strategy*)
>
> "I'm not surprised that most of you have just 20 to 40 of these points in your notes. Research shows that most students record only about 35% of the important lesson ideas. This is too bad because research also shows that the more notes students record, the better they perform on tests. Let me tell you now about a strategy you can use to increase note taking. I call it the reconstruction strategy, and it works like this: Soon after a lesson, reread your notes and try to recall or reconstruct lesson information missing from your notes. When you do, add the 'new' information to your notes. It really works. I've had students try it in my previous classes, and they report that they sometimes double the number of lesson points in notes—especially when they use the strategy with a partner." (*Introduce and sell the strategy*)
>
> "Let's have everyone practice the reconstruction strategy now in pairs by working through your notes from today. In a while, we'll see how more complete your notes are. I'll get you started by modeling how I would use the strategy using the first few lines of Amy's notes." (*Perfect the strategy*)
>
> "The Reconstruction Strategy, of course, is useful for any history lesson or for lessons in any subject area. Try using it in your other classes." (*Generalize the strategy*)

3

Helping Students Organize

Your school library must select books to include in the library. When those books arrive, they are not laid out in a random end-to-end line along the floor, nor are they placed on shelves by color or size. They are organized in meaningful and helpful ways such as by topic and author. Once information is selected for further study (the topic of Chapter 2), it too must be organized in meaningful and helpful ways. This chapter describes organization, the second component of the SOAR model, and introduces an organizational system that can facilitate teaching and learning at any level.

Suppose you are asked to learn the list of 12 words shown in Exhibit 3.1. If you are like most students you'll try to memorize the words one by one by repeating them over and over: "lawn mower, lawn mower, lawn mower, lawn mower . . . , spoon, spoon, spoon, spoon . . ." Rehearsing information is not, however, an effective memorization technique. Nor is rehearsal an effective problem-solving technique. To see why, take a look at the word problem in Exhibit 3.2 where you are asked to determine what disease Mr. Young has. Clearly, rehearsing the given information does not yield a solution.

The key to memorizing in the first case and to problem solving in the second case is the same. The key is organization. Look at Exhibit 3.3 and you'll notice that the items from Exhibit 3.1 were organized by categories according to where those items are commonly found—in a garage,

---

EXHIBIT 3.1   List of Words to Learn

Lawn mower	Saltshaker
Spoon	Hangers
Suit jacket	Tree saw
Shoes	Frying pan
Peanut butter	Shirt
Bicycle	Gasoline

EXHIBIT 3.2   Mr. Young Problem

Try to solve this problem in less than two minutes.

1. The man with asthma is in room 101.

2. Mr. Alex has cancer.

3. Mr. Osborne is in room 105.

4. Mr. Wilson has TB.

5. The man with mono is in room 104.

6. Mr. Thomas is in room 101.

7. Mr. Wilson is in room 102.

8. One of the men has epilepsy.

9. One of the patients is in room 103.

What disease does Mr. Young have?

---

kitchen, or closet. It is much easier to memorize the organized material because instead of remembering 12 distinct items you need only remember three blocks of associated items. By remembering the category garage, for example, you're likely to remember its contents: lawn mower, bicycle, tree saw, and gasoline. Look at Exhibit 3.4 and you'll notice that the information from Exhibit 3.2 was organized by patient, disease, and room. This organization allows you to solve the problem and determine that Mr. Young has mono.

EXHIBIT 3.3   Organized Words

Garage Things	Kitchen Things	Closet Things
Lawn mower	Spoon	Suit jacket
Bicycle	Peanut butter	Shoes
Tree saw	Saltshaker	Hangers
Gasoline	Frying pan	Shirt

EXHIBIT 3.4   Solution to Mr. Young Problem

Patient	Disease	Room
Thomas	Asthma	101
Alex	Cancer	103
Osborne	Epilepsy	105
Wilson	TB	102
Young	Mono	104

Students rarely organize information and instead learn in a piecemeal fashion—one idea at a time (Gubbels, 1999). Given the three types of symbiosis and their definitions shown in Exhibit 3.5, students commonly try to memorize the terms and definitions one by one, in a piecemeal fashion, as if the terms are unrelated to one another. To see just how ineffective the piecemeal approach is, consider what is done when you work a jigsaw puzzle. You assemble or organize all the pieces into a completed whole. You do not examine each piece separately—"This one has a rounded edge and is bright green with a hint of brown"—and toss it aside. To complete a puzzle or acquire information, the pieces must be organized. Returning to the symbiotic terms, Exhibit 3.6 shows how that information might be better organized in order to highlight the associations among the terms. At a glance, it is evident from Exhibit 3.6 that symbiotic relationships always involve two organisms and that one organism always benefits. The three types of symbiosis are differentiated by what happens to the second organism. It can be unaffected (commensalism), benefited (mutualism), or harmed (parasitism).

EXHIBIT 3.5   Symbiosis Terms and Definitions

Symbiosis	A situation in which two living organisms live together in a close nutritional relationship.
Commensalism	A type of symbiosis where one organism benefits and the other is unaffected.
Mutualism	A type of symbiosis where both organisms benefit.
Parasitism	A type of symbiosis where one organism benefits and the other is harmed.

EXHIBIT 3.6   Symbiosis Material Organized

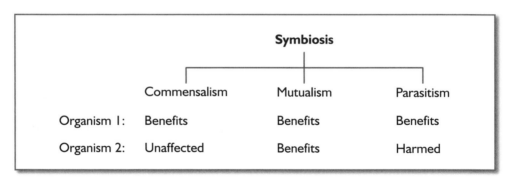

	Commensalism	Mutualism	Parasitism
Organism 1:	Benefits	Benefits	Benefits
Organism 2:	Unaffected	Benefits	Harmed

Teachers sometimes promote piecemeal learning. Imagine an instructor teaching about the skeletal system. The teacher has a replica of each bone and lays them out end to end around the room for students to examine. Examining each bone separately, however, is about as helpful as examining the pieces of a jigsaw puzzle one by one. To learn about the skeletal system, students need to see how the bones are organized to form the hand, leg, or ribcage. As another example, look at the disparate but commonly taught formulas for finding the area of four-sided polygons shown in the middle row of Exhibit 3.7. Because the formulas appear different, they are usually taught separately in a piecemeal fashion. Now look at the bottom row of Exhibit 3.7 and notice that the three area formulas are actually identical. In each case the formula is base times height. Because they are related, the square, rectangle, and parallelogram pieces should be grouped together when teaching about the area of four-sided polygons. When teachers present information in a piecemeal fashion, student learning is hindered. Students learn a few isolated facts but fail to learn how those facts are related.

EXHIBIT 3.7   Chart Showing Disparate and Common Area Formulas

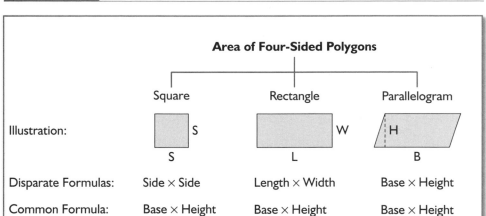

Teachers also inhibit learning when they organize information using outlines (Kiewra, 1994; Robinson & Kiewra, 1995). Yes, the outline, the long-standing bastion of organization, is actually an inferior way to organize ideas. I realize this assertion sounds ludicrous—after all, outlines have been an educational staple since the dawn of chalk and paste—but it is true. Exhibit 3.8 shows a simple outline on the subject wildcats. Notice it contains four topics (tiger, lion, cheetah, and bobcat), five categories common to all topics (call, weight, life span, habitat, and social behavior), and details pertaining to the intersection of topics and categories (e.g., the lion's weight is 400 pounds). The outline presents this information in a linear, listlike, top-to-bottom organization—much like the bones lined end to end around the classroom.

Now compare the wildcat outline to the wildcat chart (hereafter called a matrix) in Exhibit 3.9. They contain identical information, but the matrix is organized in two dimensions. Topics appear along the top, categories down the left margin, and details within the matrix cells. The matrix's two-dimensional organization is superior because it localizes, or groups, related information better than the outline (Kauffman & Kiewra, 1999). To help you understand localization, suppose you had to compare five yearbook photographs with each appearing on a different page. It is difficult to compare photographs on different pages or even if dispersed among other photographs on a single page. The photographs are not localized. Now suppose that the five photographs appeared along a single row, one after another. When the photographs are organized together—localized—they are easy to compare. Returning to the wildcat material, a student using the outline to compare the weights of wildcats to determine the heaviest has to locate the details pertaining to each wildcat's weight from four distinct sections of the outline, hold and

EXHIBIT 3.8   Wildcat Outline

Wildcats

Tiger
  Call: Roar
  Weight: 450
  Life span: 25
  Habitat: Jungle
  Social behavior: Solitary

Lion
  Call: Roar
  Weight: 400
  Life span: 25
  Habitat: Plains
  Social behavior: Groups

Cheetah
  Call: Purr
  Weight: 125
  Life span: 8
  Habitat: Plains
  Social behavior: Groups

Bobcat
  Call: Purr
  Weight: 30
  Life span: 6
  Habitat: Jungle
  Social behavior: Solitary

compare the four weights in memory, and devise a response. In contrast, the matrix localizes the four wildcat weights in a single row, making them visible in a single glance and easier to compare.

Consider another example involving information from two categories: call and weight. Students studying the Exhibit 3.8 outline top to bottom, topic by topic, probably won't notice the relationship between call and weight because this information must be gathered and synthesized from eight different and separated lines within the outline. In contrast, this same information is localized along adjacent matrix rows in Exhibit 3.9, making it easier to see the relationship that wildcats with loud calls weigh more than wildcats with soft calls. To sum up, the outline separates related material, and its linear organization encourages students to study it top to bottom, one topic at a time, so that relationships across topics are missed.

EXHIBIT 3.9	Wildcat Matrix

	Wildcats			
	Tiger	Lion	Cheetah	Bobcat
Call:	Roar	Roar	Purr	Purr
Weight:	450	400	125	30
Life span:	25	25	8	6
Habitat:	Jungle	Plains	Plains	Jungle
Social behavior:	Solitary	Groups	Groups	Solitary

The matrix localizes related material, and its two-dimensional organization encourages students to study it top to bottom and side to side so that relationships across topics are apparent (Kiewra, Kauffman, Robinson, DuBois, & Staley, 1999).

Information is often presented to students in less than optimal ways—in blocks of text, in outlines, in lists, and in bite-size pieces. These organizations commonly obscure relationships inherent in the presented material. They hide kitchen things, Mr. Young's disease, symbiotic relationships, the completed puzzle, the skeletal structure of the hand, common formulas for the areas of polygons, relationships among wildcats, and similarities and differences among photographed faces. Whenever possible, teachers should organize information in ways that highlight associations among presented ideas as was done in Exhibits 3.3, 3.4, 3.6, 3.7, and 3.9. The next section of this chapter introduces you to the Representational System designed to highlight relationships.

THE REPRESENTATIONAL SYSTEM

Representations show relationships. My colleague, Nelson Dubois, and I (Kiewra, 1994; Kiewra & DuBois, 1998) developed a simple representation system that organizes information into one or more of the following patterns: hierarchy, sequence, matrix, and illustration. Each type of representation organizes information in a unique way and reveals a unique type of relationship. Exhibit 3.10 is a representation showing the four types of

EXHIBIT 3.10   The Representational System

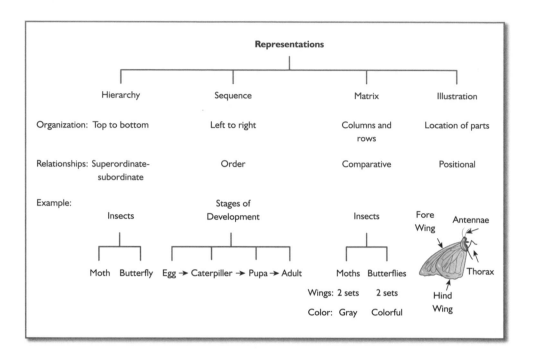

representations. As you can see, in the leftmost column of Exhibit 3.10, a *hierarchy* organizes information in a top-to-bottom fashion and reveals superordinate–subordinate relationships. In the example, the moth and butterfly are subordinate to the superordinate insects. The next column to the right pertains to the sequence representation. A *sequence* organizes information in a left-to-right fashion and reveals order relationships. In the example, the ordering of developmental stages for moths and butterflies is shown. The next column to the right pertains to the matrix representation. A *matrix* organizes information in columns and rows (or by topics and categories) and reveals comparative relationships. In the insects matrix example, the wings and color for moths and butterflies are easily compared. The right-most column of Exhibit 3.10 pertains to *illustration* representations. These are organized according to the locations of parts and reveal positional relationships. In the illustration example, the relative locations of insect body parts are shown. Next, each representation pattern is examined in more detail.

Hierarchy

A hierarchy organizes information top to bottom to reveal superordinate–subordinate relationships. Exhibit 3.11 shows a hierarchy for musical instruments. You'll notice, among other things, these hierarchical relationships: There are four superordinate types of instruments—brass, wind,

EXHIBIT 3.11   Musical Instruments Hierarchy

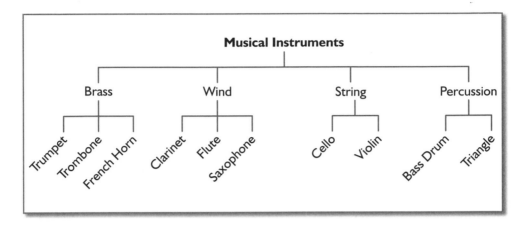

string, and percussion; trumpet, trombone, and French horn are types of brass instruments; and cello and violin are types of string instruments.

Exhibit 3.12 shows another sample hierarchy for birds. Note that there are three main types of birds—raptors, waterbirds, and songbirds; two types of raptors—eagles and hawks; and two types of eagles—bald and golden. Note, too, that songbirds are superordinate to sparrows and thrushes, and that trumpeter and black are subordinate to swans.

You might be surprised to realize how much information is organized hierarchically. Here are just a few examples: a family tree, corporations, military personnel, parts of the body, animals, food groups, types of literature, types of numbers, artistic styles, models of cars, and even the cosmos.

EXHIBIT 3.12   Birds Hierarchy

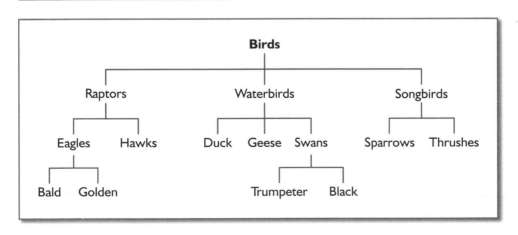

Tips for Constructing Hierarchies

1. Always construct hierarchies top to bottom so that superordinate–subordinate relationships are clear. Later, you'll see that this top-to-bottom organization is essential for combining hierarchies with other representations.

2. Be alert for certain words (alert words, I call them) signaling that information is organized hierarchically. When you see or hear these words, information is related in a superordinate–subordinate fashion and a hierarchy is the appropriate representation.

Sample hierarchy alert words are shown in the leftmost column of Exhibit 3.13.

EXHIBIT 3.13	Sample Alert Words for Hierarchy, Sequence, Matrix, and Illustration Representations

Hierarchy	Sequence	Matrix	Illustration
Parts	Steps	Compare	Parts of things
Types	Phases	Contrast	Cerebrum
Components	Stages	However	Cerebellum
Elements	Develop	Whereas	Appearance of things
Characteristics	Process	Similar	Scaly
Levels	Period	Different	Smooth
Groups	First	Alternative	Location of things
Aspects	Later	Early	Above
Kinds	Next	Domestic	Top right

Here are some examples of alert words and resulting hierarchies:

• There are four *components* to the SOAR model: select, organize, associate, and regulate.

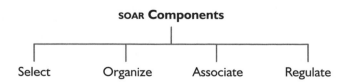

- There are four *types* of measurement: nominal, ordinal, interval, and ratio.

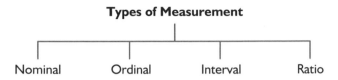

- There are three *kinds* of levers: first, second, and third.

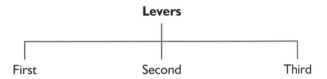

- Atoms *contain* protons, neutrons, and electrons.

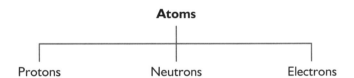

3. Include all levels. A hierarchy is more accurate and informative when it displays all the important levels of information. Exhibit 3.14 is a poorly constructed hierarchy because it shows types of punctuation as single-level hierarchy. Examining it, you would simply believe there are seven unique types of punctuation. That belief is wrong. Now examine the multilevel hierarchy for punctuation (Exhibit 3.15). This hierarchy is more accurate and informative because it groups types of punctuation. It shows that the seven types of punctuation belong to the larger families of end-of-sentence punctuation or within-sentence punctuation. Similarly, if asked to create a hierarchy for major league baseball teams, you would not create a single-level hierarchy showing all 30 teams. Instead, you would create a multilevel hierarchy showing that baseball teams are first divided into the American League and National League and then into Eastern, Central, and Western divisions. Remember this piece of advice when creating hierarchies: See if information appearing at the same level can be further grouped. If so, additional hierarchical levels are needed.

EXHIBIT 3.14   Poorly Constructed Single-Level Punctuation Hierarchy

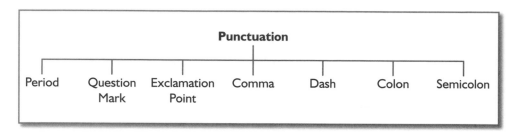

EXHIBIT 3.15   Well Constructed Multilevel Punctuation Hierarchy

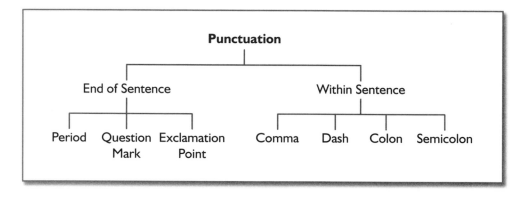

Sequence

A sequence organizes information left to right to reveal order relationships—what comes first, second, third, and so on—with arrows pointing left to right between each step in the sequence. Exhibit 3.16 shows a sequence representation for the process of digestion. Reading it left to right, it is easy to see the order of locations that food travels during digestion. Exhibit 3.17 shows a sequence representation for calculating standard deviation. It indicates the five steps required in this order: calculate deviation scores, square deviation scores, sum deviation scores, divide sum by the number of scores, and find square root of quotient.

Much of what is taught and learned can be represented sequentially. For example, the plot of a story, artistic periods, the procedure for a scientific experiment, the developmental stages of morality, the migratory patterns of birds, the water cycle, the process of photosynthesis, and historical events are all represented sequentially.

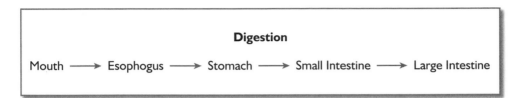

EXHIBIT 3.16   Digestion Sequence

Digestion

Mouth ⟶ Esophogus ⟶ Stomach ⟶ Small Intestine ⟶ Large Intestine

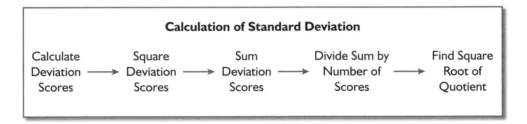

EXHIBIT 3.17   Sequence for Calculation of Standard Deviation

Calculation of Standard Deviation

Calculate Deviation Scores	Square Deviation Scores	Sum Deviation Scores	Divide Sum by Number of Scores	Find Square Root of Quotient

Tips for Constructing Sequences

1. Always construct sequences left to right and place arrows between steps. Again, this organization is necessary for combining sequences with other representations.

2. Be on guard for certain alert words signaling that information is organized sequentially. When you see or hear these words, information occurs in a certain order and a sequence representation is appropriate. Sample alert words are shown in the second column of Exhibit 3.13.

Here are some examples of sequence alert words and representations:

- Piaget's *stages* of development

Piaget's Stages of Development

Sensorimotor → Preoperational → Concrete → Formal

- The Renaissance *period followed* the Classical *period.*

Periods

Classical → Renaissance

- The *phases* of the moon.

Moon Phases

New → First Quarter → Full → Last Quarter

- The life *cycle* of the butterfly.

Butterfly Life Cycle

Egg → Caterpillar → Pupa → Adult

3. Include all levels. Just as some hierarchies have multiple levels, some sequences do too. Examine the sequence for adding mixed fractions in Exhibit 3.18. Notice that it does not contain one level with nine steps but two levels with the upper level showing that there are four overriding phases to adding mixed fractions. Just as it was easier at the outset of Chapter 3 to learn the list of 12 words when organized into three categories (e.g., kitchen things), it is also easier to learn the nine steps for adding mixed fractions when organized into four overriding phases.

EXHIBIT 3.18 Well-Constructed Multilevel Sequence

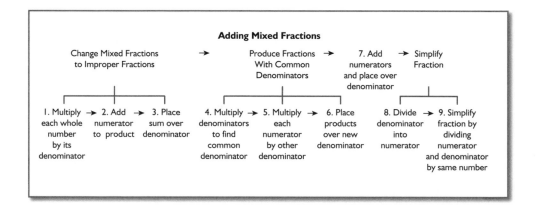

Matrix

A matrix organizes information in columns and rows to reveal comparative relationships. A matrix can show relationships within and across topics. Examine the matrix on young marriage in Exhibit 3.19 and look for relationships within topics (within the columns) and across topics (across the rows). Some within-topic relationships include the following:

- When marriage partners drop out of high school, become pregnant before marriage, and are younger than 18 years of age the marriage success rate is poor.

• When marriage partners are at least 18 years old (female) and 20 (male) years old, graduate high school, and delay pregnancy for at least one year after marriage, the marriage success rate is high.

Some across-topic relationships include the following:

• The probability for a successful marriage increases as age increases.

• High school graduates have more successful marriages than high school dropouts.

• The success of a marriage depends, in part, on delaying pregnancy. Marriages with pregnancies before marriage have the worst success rate; marriages with pregnancies at least one year after marriage have the best success rate.

EXHIBIT 3.19   Young Marriage Matrix

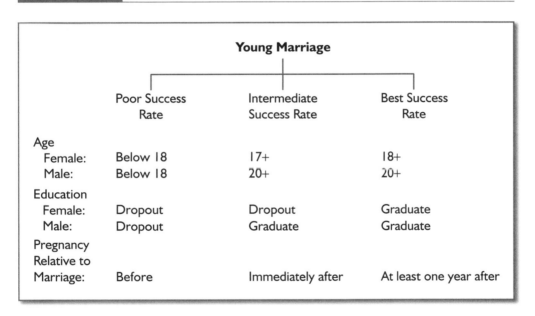

	Poor Success Rate	Intermediate Success Rate	Best Success Rate
Young Marriage			
Age			
Female:	Below 18	17+	18+
Male:	Below 18	20+	20+
Education			
Female:	Dropout	Dropout	Graduate
Male:	Dropout	Graduate	Graduate
Pregnancy Relative to Marriage:	Before	Immediately after	At least one year after

Another matrix example pertaining to moths and butterflies appears in Exhibit 3.20. The following comparative relationships, among others, are evident:

• The moth has two sets of wings that are folded down at rest (within topic).

• The moth has a dull color, which is just as well because it flies at night when it cannot be seen (within topic).

• Moths and butterflies progress through the same four developmental stages (across topic).

- Moths and butterflies both have two sets of wings (across topic).

- Moths seem introverted—their wings are folded down, they have feathery antennae, they are a dull color, and they fly at night when no one can see them. In contrast, butterflies seem extroverted—their wings are outstretched, they have long and zany antennae with knobs, they are brightly colored, and they fly during the day when they can show off their wild appearance (across topic).

Matrices are the ideal representation for comparing two or more things. Already in this text, you have seen matrices used to compare planets, teaching and learning effectiveness, the results of experiments, types of symbiosis, area formulas for polygons, types of wildcats, types of representations, young marriage success rates, and moths and butterflies. Other examples might include representations comparing historical events, types of stars, political candidates, fictional characters, parts of speech, styles of poetry, musical or artistic periods, string instruments, Greek and Roman gods, architectural designs, acids and bases, types of muscle, investment options, body organs, and defense strategies. In fact, try to come up with an instance when a comparison is not possible. World War I can be compared with World War II, the Trojan War with the Korean Conflict, cumulus clouds with cirrus clouds, Fahrenheit with centigrade, rational numbers with real numbers, Mozart with Beethoven, Abbott with Costello, and Avis with Hertz. Matrices can be used to compare anything.

EXHIBIT 3.20   Moths and Butterflies Matrix

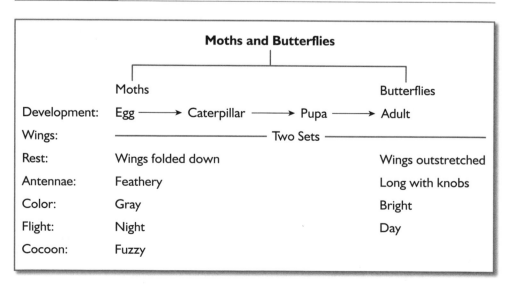

Tips for Constructing Matrices

1. Construct matrices from hierarchies and sequences. All hierarchies and sequences can be extended downward to form a matrix. This is accomplished by adding categories down the left side and adding details to the matrix cells at the intersection of topics and categories. For example, Exhibit 3.21 is a matrix comparing types of punctuation. It is an extension of the hierarchy that appeared earlier in Exhibit 3.15. Exhibit 3.22 is a matrix comparing the stages of digestion. It is an extension of the digestion sequence that appeared earlier in Exhibit 3.16.

EXHIBIT 3.21   Punctuation Matrix Extended From Hierarchy

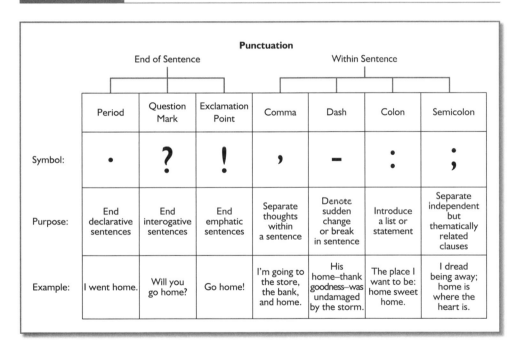

EXHIBIT 3.22   Digestion Matrix Extended From Sequence

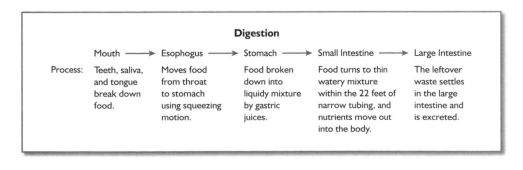

2. Construct matrices with three parts: the topics that appear on top as part of a hierarchy or sequence, the categories down the left side, and the details that appear in the matrix cells at the intersection of topics and categories. Exhibit 3.23 is a matrix depicting the matrix parts in terms of location and description.

EXHIBIT 3.23 Matrix Showing Matrix Parts

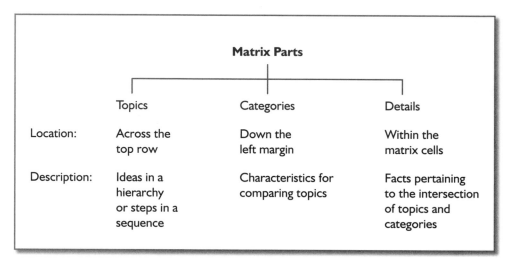

3. Be on guard for alert words signaling a comparative relationship. When you hear or see these words, information is comparative and best organized in a matrix. Sample alert words are shown in the third column of Exhibit 3.13.

Here are sample alert words and resulting matrix frameworks:

- *Alternative* means of transportation

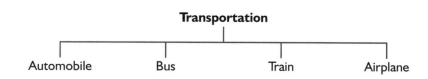

Travel time:

Cost:

• Let's *compare* the stages of development in terms of age and cognitive ability.

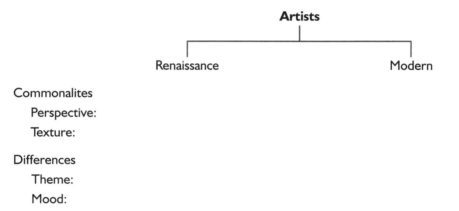

Stages of Development

Sensorimotor ⟶ Preoperational ⟶ Concrete ⟶ Formal

Age:

Cognitive ability:

• Modern artists share several *commonalities* with Renaissance artists.

Artists

Renaissance   Modern

Commonalites
  Perspective:
  Texture:

Differences
  Theme:
  Mood:

• *Breast*-feeding is recommended for babies.

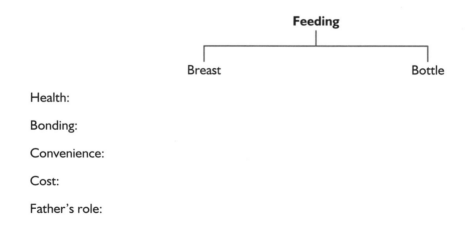

Feeding

Breast   Bottle

Health:

Bonding:

Convenience:

Cost:

Father's role:

In the above examples, alert words suggested a potential comparison among topics and the need for a matrix representation. Alert words like *alternative, compare,* and *commonalities* connote that topics can be compared to find similarities and contrasted to find differences. After all, no matter how alike things are, they must also be different. A less obvious comparative alert word is *breast*, used here to describe a type of feeding. If there is breast-feeding, then there must be other types of feeding. The same holds true for other adjectives that suggest comparative relationships. For instance, *early* explorers can be compared with later explorers, *domestic* policies with international policies, *male* viewpoints with female viewpoints, *organic* molecules with inorganic molecules, and *Supreme Court* decisions with decisions made by lower courts. Be alert for adjectives and the potential comparisons they suggest.

4. Order topics and categories. All matrices are not created equal (Kauffman, LeBow, Kiewra, & Igo, 2000; Kiewra, DuBois, Christian, McShane, Meyerhoffer, & Roskelley, 1991). Matrix representations containing identical information but varying in their order of topics or categories can differ widely in their ability to show comparative relationships. Exhibit 3.24 shows two matrices with identical information about types of prose. Matrix 1 orders the topics to capture the increasing length and complexity among the types of prose; Matrix 2 does not. Matrix 1 also orders the categories so that the related

EXHIBIT 3.24   Prose Matrix 1 and Prose Matrix 2

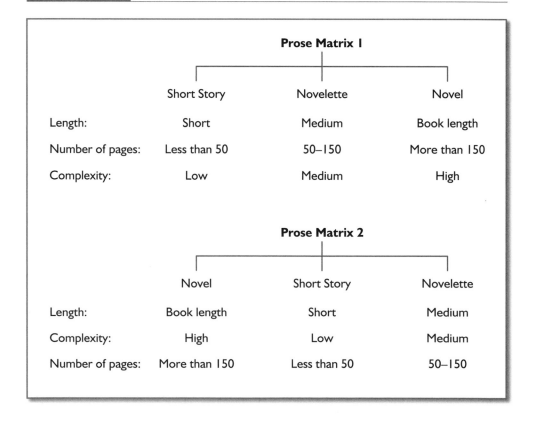

Prose Matrix 1

	Short Story	Novelette	Novel
Length:	Short	Medium	Book length
Number of pages:	Less than 50	50–150	More than 150
Complexity:	Low	Medium	High

Prose Matrix 2

	Novel	Short Story	Novelette
Length:	Book length	Short	Medium
Complexity:	High	Low	Medium
Number of pages:	More than 150	Less than 50	50–150

categories, length and number of pages, are consecutive; Matrix 2 does not. Consequently, Matrix 1 clearly shows the increasing length and complexity of prose going from short story to novelette to novel. Matrix 2 obscures this comparative relationship. Remember to order topics and categories in ways that highlight relationships.

Illustration

An illustration represents information pictorially and reveals positional relationships. It shows what something looks like, its parts, and the relative position of those parts. Exhibit 3.25 is an illustration of a flower and its parts. Exhibit 3.26 is an illustration of the brain and its major parts.

Illustrations are useful across almost any subject area. In science, they can be used to illustrate the digestive process, the parts of a cell, or the force placed on an object. In social studies, they can be used to illustrate ancient pyramids, primitive tools, or geographical formations such as inlets and mountain ranges. In mathematics, illustrations can depict geometric figures like parallelograms and cubes. In physical education, they can help players learn positions and tactics (such as how to run a weave play in basketball).

Illustrations can be used alone or in conjunction with other representations—hierarchies, sequences, and matrices. A hierarchy for types of leaves can be extended into a matrix with the category *appearance* that includes illustrations of the different leaves. Similarly, a sequence for the life cycle of a butterfly can be extended into a matrix with the category

EXHIBIT 3.25 Flower Illustration

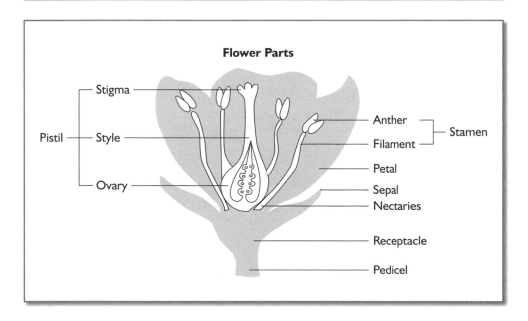

EXHIBIT 3.26 Illustration of the Brain

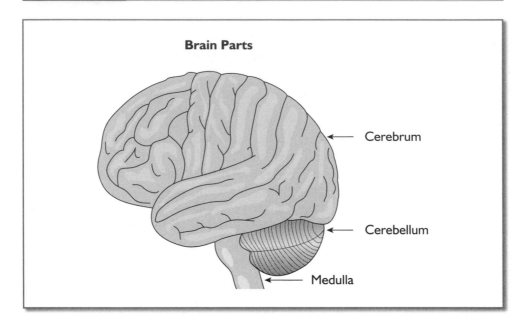

Brain Parts

Cerebrum

Cerebellum

Medulla

appearance that includes illustrations of egg, larvae, pupa, and adult. Exhibit 3.27 shows a fish matrix that includes illustrations of the fish. The illustrations help learners understand the direct relationship between a fish's appearance and where it hides from predators or prey.

EXHIBIT 3.27 Fish Matrix That Includes Illustration

	Fish			
	Crappie	Catfish	Croaker	Albacore
Illustration:				
Appearance:	Mottled	Dark upper side	Vertical stripes	Light-colored belly
Purpose:	Hide in rocks or bottom	Hard to see from above	Hide in vegetation	Hard to see from below
Habitat:	Bottom	Bottom	Vegetation	Surface

Tips for Constructing Illustrations

1. Keep it simple. Although illustrations show what things look like, they are representations not exact replicas. Include only the details needed and don't worry about how realistic things look. An illustration is effective if it shows what it intends to show. For instance, the illustration of the brain in Exhibit 3.26 is simple but effective. As intended, it illustrates the brain's major parts and their relative size and position.

2. Use labels and captions to explain illustrations (Mayer, 1997). The flower illustration in Exhibit 3.25 and the brain illustration in 3.26 both contain labels marking their parts and captions explaining the illustration. Whenever possible, place labels and captions close to their referents so that relationships are easily made between words and pictures. When information that belongs together is not localized—as you saw previously with outlines—learning is diminished.

3. Be alert for certain words signaling a positional relationship. These are words that refer to parts, appearance, or location of things as shown in the rightmost column of Exhibit 3.13.

Here are some alert words and resulting illustrations:

• When the ball is *moved up* the *left side,* the *right wing* should be positioned *at* the *right post.*

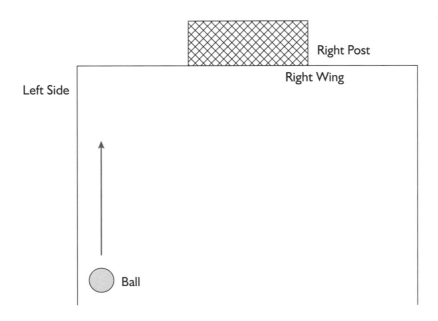

- The king in chess can *move one square* in *any direction* to eight possible squares.

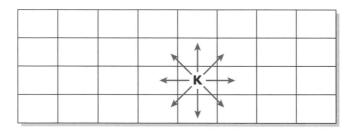

- Killer whales have a *triangular* dorsal fin *located on* their *middle back*. The male's fin is *larger* and *more upright* than the female's.

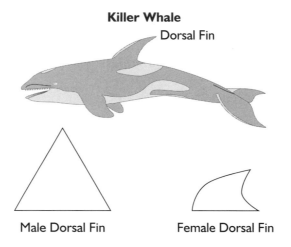

Killer Whale

Dorsal Fin

Male Dorsal Fin   Female Dorsal Fin

HELPING STUDENTS ORGANIZE INFORMATION

The Representational System, just described, can be used by teachers in three ways to improve instruction and learning. First, it can be used to plan lessons. A teacher who needs to teach a lesson about flowers might first construct the flower illustration presented earlier in Exhibit 3.25 and construct the new flower matrix shown in Exhibit 3.28. The matrix displays the flower's three main structures, parts, and subparts as well as the appearance, location, and function of each. Imagine trying to teach this lesson without first creating the flower illustration and matrix.

Second, organized materials can be shared with students. For example, the flower materials used to plan instruction can also be given to students to make sure they have a complete and organized set of study notes. A teacher instructing students about levers created the matrix representation in Exhibit 3.29 and shared it with students.

EXHIBIT 3.28 Flower Matrix

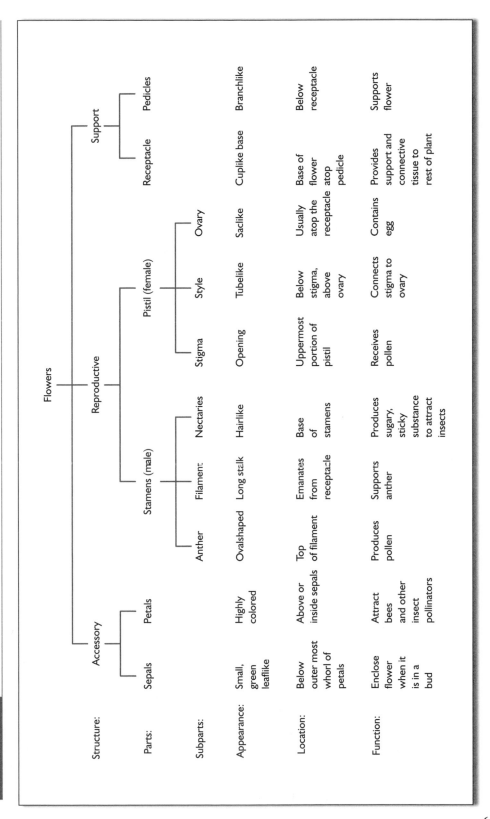

Structure:	Accessory		Reproductive								Support	
Parts:	Sepals	Petals	Stamens (male)			Pistil (female)					Receptacle	Pedicles
Subparts:			Anther	Filament	Nectaries	Stigma	Style	Ovary				
Appearance:	Small, green leaflike	Highly colored	Ovalshaped	Long stalk	Hairlike	Opening	Tubelike	Saclike	Cuplike base	Branchlike		
Location:	Below outer most whorl of petals	Above or inside sepals	Top of filament	Emanates from receptacle	Base of stamens	Uppermost portion of pistil	Below stigma, above ovary	Usually atop the receptacle	Base of flower atop pedicle	Below receptacle		
Function:	Enclose flower when it is in a bud	Attract bees and other insect pollinators	Produces pollen	Supports anther	Produces sugary, sticky substance to attract insects	Receives pollen	Connects stigma to ovary	Contains egg	Provides support and connective tissue to rest of plant	Supports flower		

61

EXHIBIT 3.29   Levers Matrix

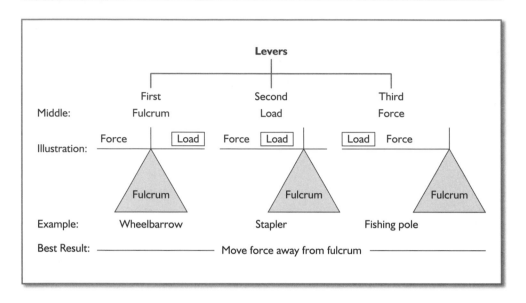

If you believe students should have a hand in creating their own study notes, you can give them a matrix framework, like that seen in Exhibit 3.30 on the subject of clouds. A matrix framework (first introduced in Chapter 2) presents the lesson topics and categories and provides space within the matrix cells to record details that intersect topics and categories. Frameworks probably work best when associated with organizational

EXHIBIT 3.30   Clouds Matrix

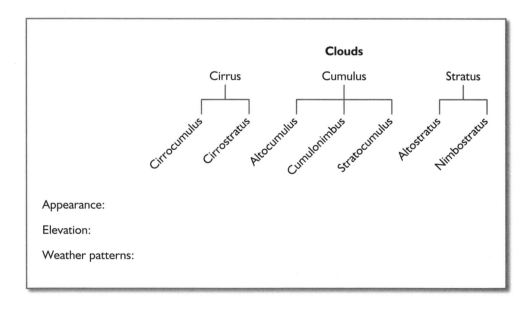

cues (also introduced in Chapter 2). A cue such as "Now, let's discuss the *weather patterns* associated with *cumulus* clouds" alerts students to the particular matrix cell now addressed.

Last, teachers can teach students how to organize information by teaching them the Representational System. Recall that strategies are best taught by embedding them within content instruction. Below is an example of how a teacher might embed organizational strategy instruction in a lesson on operant conditioning.

STRATEGY INSTRUCTION: TEACHING STUDENTS TO ORGANIZE

"Class, I've given you a sheet (Exhibit 3.31) containing the four terms and definitions you'll need to learn for our lesson on operant conditioning. While teaching you about operant conditioning, I'm also going to teach you a strategy that you'll find helpful for organizing this information and, really, any information that involves comparing two or more things." (*Introduce and generalize the strategy*)

"As you look at the sheet, you'll notice that there are four terms and definitions. Most students try to learn this information by repeating the terms and definitions over and over, 'Positive reinforcement: presentation of a stimulus following a behavior that increases that behavior. Positive reinforcement: presentation of a stimulus following a behavior that increases that behavior. Positive reinforcement . . .' This won't work. Repetition does not produce long-term memorization and it certainly does not produce understanding." (*Sell the strategy*)

EXHIBIT 3.31   Operant Conditioning Terms and Definitions

Positive reinforcement	Presentation of a stimulus following a behavior that increases that behavior.
Negative reinforcement	Removal of a stimulus following a behavior that increases that behavior.
Positive punishment	Presentation of a stimulus following a behavior that decreases that behavior.
Negative punishment	Removal of a stimulus following a behavior that decreases that behavior.

"Instead you need to see how these terms are alike and different. Without even reading the definitions, you know that positive reinforcement and negative reinforcement are alike because both involve reinforcement. Now read the definitions and see just how they are alike. That's right, they both *increase* behavior. Given that reinforcement increases behavior, predict what punishment does. You think it decreases behavior? Look at the punishment definitions and see . . . you're right. Punishment *decreases* behavior." (*Sell the strategy*)

"Back to reinforcement: There are two types—positive and negative. These must be different because they have different names. Read to see how they are different. That's correct; the stimulus is *presented* for positive reinforcement and *removed* for negative reinforcement. Without reading further, predict how positive punishment and negative punishment differ. That's right; just as was true for reinforcement, the stimulus is *presented* for positive punishment and *removed* for negative punishment. All in all, you've learned how these four operant conditioning terms are related: Reinforcement terms involve an increase in behavior; punishment terms involve a decrease in behavior. Positive terms involve the presentation of a stimulus and negative terms involve the removal of a stimulus." (*Sell the strategy*)

"Now that we got that sorted out, I'm going to show you how to construct a matrix representation that easily shows the nifty relationships we just discovered among the operant terms. Take a look as I create the matrix on the board (Exhibit 3.32). I begin with the title *operant conditioning*. Then, I make two arms coming down to show the two main types: *reinforcement* and *punishment*. Each of these has an arm coming down to show that their subtypes can be

EXHIBIT 3.32   Operant Conditioning Matrix

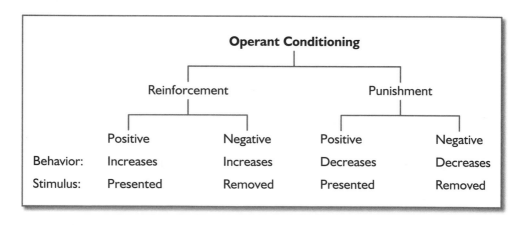

positive or *negative.* Then, I add categories that relate to these terms in the left margin. The categories are *behavior* and *stimulus.* Inside the matrix cells, I add the details that intersect the subtopics (positive reinforcement and negative reinforcement, and positive punishment and negative punishment) along the top and the categories (behavior and stimulus) down the side. The details can be examined independently (e.g., positive reinforcement involves the presentation of a stimulus) or collectively to reveal important relationships (e.g., negative techniques involve the removal of a stimulus)." (*Introduce and sell the strategy*)

"A matrix representation can be used any time you need to compare things. Later, we'll cover four schedules for reinforcement and you'll get practice constructing a matrix that compares the schedules. We'll also be studying learning theories other than operant conditioning so you'll have the chance to construct a matrix that compares the various theories." (*Perfect and generalize the strategy*)

4

Helping Students Associate

Learning depends on *selecting* important information and *organizing* it as best possible. But soaring to success does not end there. Well organized information is just a pretty picture, unless it is associated. In this chapter you'll learn (a) the importance of association, (b) that memory experts use association, (c) types of association, (d) implications for building associations, and (e) how to teach students to create associations.

THE IMPORTANCE OF ASSOCIATION

Let's begin with a little memory quiz. We'll see how well you remember things that you experience frequently. Write out your answers to each question or problem below before checking your answers in Exhibit 4.1.

- Draw the calling pad of a push button telephone. Include all numbers, letters, and symbols associated with each of the 12 main keys. No checking your cell phone for help!
- Sketch the playing card the six of hearts. No fair flipping to one of the 15 channels broadcasting a poker game.
- You know that George Washington is pictured on the dollar bill, but do you know if Washington is turned to the left, facing straight ahead, or turned to the right as you look at the bill? And for you rich folks, "Yes, the dollar bill is still in circulation!"

EXHIBIT 4.1 Memory Quiz Answers

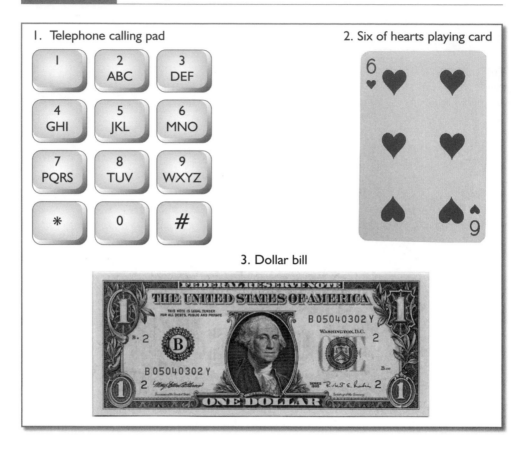

How did you do? Assuming you're like most people—except much better looking—then you made errors on most or all of these tasks. Perhaps you mistakenly placed letters on the telephone's *one* key or omitted some letters from the *seven* and *nine* keys. You probably drew a blank recalling that the six of hearts has eight hearts and their locations. And you were probably surprised to see ol' George turned to the right.

All in all, you are probably dismayed by your weak memory for these things, given the frequency you are exposed to them. Here's the problem: Even frequent and long-term exposure does not necessarily produce an accurate memory (Neisser, 1982). Just as hanging around a gym does not make you fit, repeated exposure to information does not make you knowledgeable. And yet many students simply show up for class hoping exposure to the teacher's words expands their minds with knowledge. They mindlessly mouth the words from their textbooks hoping they become imprinted in their brains. Others are even more optimistic. They tuck their books beneath their pillows at night and dream that text ideas permeate their gray matter through osmosis. Research (Gubbels, 1999; Van Meter, Yokoi, & Pressley, 1994) confirms that students use a host of redundant strategies meant to expose them to information again and again. They reread, rehearse, recopy, and recite . . . ridiculous! When students "study" class notes, for example, 12% report they do nothing more than recopy notes verbatim. About 50% report reviewing notes (Gubbels, 1999). Most reviewers, though, passively recite noted ideas word for word.

Many students and teachers mistakenly view education as the accumulation of independent facts through repeated exposure to those facts. For example, Exhibit 4.2 is a list of facts about rhinos that a teacher might present to students who, in turn, will try to learn them by reciting them over and over: The white rhino has square lips. The white rhino has square lips. The problem with this piecemeal and redundant approach to learning is that the facts are easily confused or forgotten because they seem arbitrary and nonmeaningful. For example, the student (and perhaps the teacher) does not know why the white rhino has square lips so the student might forget this information or mistakenly recall that the white rhino has hooked lips.

If repeated exposure is not the key to learning rhino or other facts, then what is? The answer is association (Mayer, 1984, 1996). By associating the ideas being learned to one another and to ideas outside the material, meaningful learning occurs. Reexamine the list of rhino facts found in Exhibit 4.2 and create associations. You might have noted the following associations:

- Living on the plains is associated with grass eating because grass grows on the plains.
- Living in the jungle is associated with twig eating because twigs are available in the jungle.
- Square lips are well suited for (and associated with) scooping grass.
- Hooked lips are well suited for (and associated with) grasping twigs.
- White rhinos blend in (and are associated) with light colored grasses on the plains.
- Black rhinos blend in (and are associated) with dark colored jungle habitats.
- White rhinos are associated with cows because both live on the plains, eat grass, and have square lips.

EXHIBIT 4.2   Rhino Facts

White Rhino

- Square lips
- Lives on prairie
- Eats grass

Black Rhino

- Hooked lips
- Lives in jungle
- Eats twigs

By making associations, the information is no longer arbitrary or independent and is more easily learned. We simply remember that both black and white rhinos live in habitats where they are camouflaged (black in jungles and white on the plains), eat food available to them in their habitat (black eat twigs and white eat grass), and have lips well suited for the food they eat (black have hooked lips to grasp twigs and white have square lips to scoop grass). To further make the case that association works, evidence from the study of memory experts is presented next.

MEMORY EXPERTS USE ASSOCIATION

In 1981, Rajan Mahadevan showed the world that having a prodigious memory was as easy as pi. Pi, you might recall, is the Greek letter symbolizing the ratio between the diameter and circumference of a circle. To most of us, pi is 3.14, but pi's decimal digits expand forever with no known pattern making it a favorite test for memory. Rajan set what was then the world record by faultlessly reciting 31,811 pi digits. That's a lot of pi! (The latest record is now 100,000 pi digits!)

Rajan is a quick learner when it comes to numbers. When given a six by six matrix containing single digit numbers, he can memorize the 36 numbers in about two minutes, and then, recall the matrix from memory in any direction without error. How is this possible; does Rajan have a photographic memory? Psychologist Anders Ericsson (2003), who studies superior memory, says there is no credible evidence for Rajan, or anyone, having a photographic memory. Rajan learns and remembers the numbers by making associations. For example, he recalls the consecutive numbers 8, 2, and 0 by thinking about an embarrassing incident that happened to him at 8:20 that morning. The sequence 3-1-2 reminds him of the area code for Chicago. He recalls the number sequence 1-1-1 as a "Nelson" because that's what you call a score of 111 in the game of cricket. The numbers 1, 7, 4, and 5 are remembered as the simpler 39 because Rajan somehow knows that Ben Franklin was 39 in 1745. Looking down adjacent columns, Rajan notices the consecutive numbers 17, 16, and 33 and remembers this pattern because 17 and 16 sum to 33.

Memory expert Harry Lorayne (1985) often appeared as a guest on the *Tonight Show,* starring Johnny Carson. Before the show, he would briefly meet 50 people in the audience who told him their names. During the show, those 50 people stood up and Lorayne recalled each of their names without error. How did he so quickly learn 50 names and faces? He used association, of course. He associated the name to a word or phrase that sounded similar (what he called a *zip name*), identified a distinguishing facial feature, and then visually associated the zip name and the facial feature. For example, you meet Mr. Caruthers and notice he has a high forehead.

Caruthers sounds like car udders so you imagine cars with udders driving across that forehead and you're milking the cars. The next time you see that high forehead, you'll remember the cars with udders and remember the name Caruthers. Perhaps, it's best not to mention your name learning technique to Mr. Caruthers! My own name, Kiewra, sounds like "key" and "rah." I have slightly elongated earlobes that rest comfortably on my shoulders. You might imagine a turning key rolling up an earlobe amid cheers ("rah") from a throng of long earlobe detractors.

You need not be a memory expert to showcase a prodigious memory. You can be a waiter (Ericsson & Polson, 1988). A waiter working in Boulder, Colorado, could remember orders for up to 20 customers without writing down their orders—a feat often rewarded with large gratuities. The waiter, J. C., revealed his memory strategy for other servers and memory connoisseurs. His memory tip: associations. First, J. C. "recorded" orders in groups of four people. For each person in the group, he associated the ordered entrée with some distinctive part of the person's face. He might, for example, imagine the Big Boulder steak filling the oversized jowls of a customer. The association made between entrée and facial feature was foolproof against enterprising customers who sometimes changed seats after the order was placed hoping to throw J. C.'s memory a curve when he served their food. To remember salad dressings, each was associated with a standard code letter such as B for blue cheese, O for oil and vinegar, T for Thousand Island, F for French, and so on. If the four salad dressings among a group of four were, for example, blue cheese (B), oil and vinegar (O), oil and vinegar (O), and French (F), they would be associated to form the "word" BOOF. J. C. used similar association strategies to remember the customer's side dish and specifications for cooking the meat. Personally, I'd be content to have a waiter who remembered to fill my water glass occasionally.

Of course, anyone can create associations to foster learning and memory. I've often used sports information to remember numerical data. Locker combinations have been linked to Yankee jersey numbers, pin numbers to Yankee championships. Birthdates and historical dates can also become associations. Many readers, I'm sure, have used their birthdates as passwords or pin numbers: a surefire way to bolster memory and suffer identity theft. There can also be pros and cons to using historical dates as this next story attests.

It was my sophomore year of college at Oneonta—a small college in upstate New York with a disproportionate number of vowels. My roommate, Houser, and I were visiting our friend, Lyle, at the start of the fall semester, when Lyle announced that he had a new phone number. "Fire away," I said, "I'll jot it down." "You won't need to write this number down," Lyle replied smugly, "I came up with a great way to remember it: Columbus minus 2." "Columbus minus two," I echoed, "What are you talking about?" "Well, everyone knows that Columbus sailed the ocean blue in 1492. Subtract two from that historic date and you have my new phone number—1490, plus the standard Oneonta prefix . . . 432. I learned all about memory techniques in my educational psychology course," Lyle remarked with an air of mnemonic superiority. "Wow, that's great," I said admiringly, yet unaware that the door to my educational psychology future had just cracked open.

Houser, meanwhile, was not impressed. He slinked off to a corner of the room and sat complacently with furrowed brow. Houser was a history major and the most competitive person I'd ever met. I knew that he would not let Lyle one-up-him when it came to linking phone numbers to historical dates. Sure enough, Houser strode proudly back to Lyle and me and delivered his proclamation: "Our new phone number is also easy to remember. It's 'Magellan plus five.' You just add five to the year that Magellan sailed around the world." "Oh, that's a memorable one, Houser," Lyle replied rolling his eyes.

Unfortunately, the story does not end there. Late that very night, I was downtown on the rain-soaked Oneonta streets after closing down the city library—as we liked to call it. I didn't want to brave the long, wet walk back to campus, so I set out to do what any car-less college student would do in the middle of the night—call my roommate for a lift. I ambled to a payphone and dropped in a dime but soon realized that I had not learned our new phone number. And then it hit me like a slighted Portuguese explorer, "Magellan plus five." My dry return to campus depended on knowing when Magellan sailed around the world. So, I meekly asked passersby, "Uh, excuse me, would you happen to know when Magellan sailed around the world? No, really, it's a serious question!" Needless to say, it was a long, wet walk back to campus. The all-too-obvious point of this story: If you make an association to help remember something, be sure the association has nothing to do with Magellan.

INTERNAL AND EXTERNAL ASSOCIATIONS

Teachers can help students learn and remember new information through two types of associations: internal and external (Mayer, 1996) as shown in Exhibit 4.3. The right portion of Exhibit 4.3 shows a page of text with several key ideas (the Xs). The broken lines connecting the Xs are internal associations. They are called internal associations because they link ideas *within* the material presented. The solid lines represent external associations. These are links that extend *outside* the material being learned to information already stored in memory—as depicted by the triangles. Returning to the rhino material presented earlier, the associations between the black rhino's color and habitat (black rhinos live in dark colored jungles where they can hide), food and habitat (they eat twigs, which are abundant in the jungle), and lips and food (they have hooked lips to grasp twigs) are all examples of internal associations. The link made between the white rhino and cow (both live in grasslands and scoop grass with square-shaped lips) is an example of an external association.

EXHIBIT 4.3 Internal and External Associations

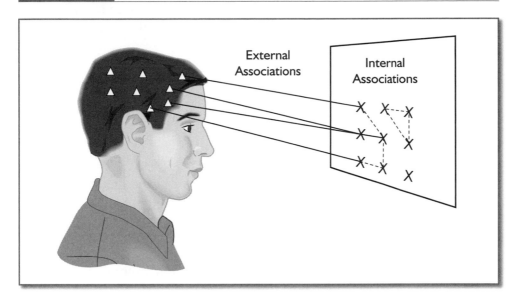

Here is another example of internal and external associations. Suppose you were teaching students the information about the nervous system and endocrine system found in the matrix in Exhibit 4.4. You could point out the following internal and external associations.

EXHIBIT 4.4 Matrix Representation for Nervous and Endocrine Systems

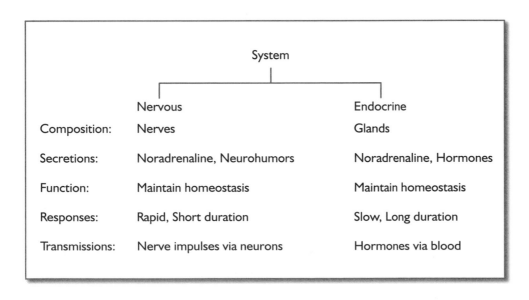

	Nervous	Endocrine
Composition:	Nerves	Glands
Secretions:	Noradrenaline, Neurohumors	Noradrenaline, Hormones
Function:	Maintain homeostasis	Maintain homeostasis
Responses:	Rapid, Short duration	Slow, Long duration
Transmissions:	Nerve impulses via neurons	Hormones via blood

Internal Associations

- The nervous system has nerves; the endocrine system has glands.
- Both systems secrete noradrenalin. Nerves also secrete neuro-humors; glands also secrete hormones.
- Nerves and glands maintain homeostasis.
- Nerves act rapidly with short duration; glands act slowly with long duration.
- Nerves travel through neurons; hormones travel through blood.

External Associations

- Nerves are like light switches turning on and off quickly.
- The pain of touching a hot stove travels through nerves.
- Remember that nerves secrete neurohumors and travel through neurons because they all begin with the letter "N." Also, "neuro" deals with nerves—like a neurologist.
- In boxing: Nerves are quick, little jabs; glands are big, slow upper-cuts that produce long effects.
- Remember that glands secrete hormones by imagining a horse (sounds like hormone) with swollen glands in its neck.

To recap, internal associations relate presented ideas with one another; external associations relate presented ideas to previous ideas and experiences already stored in memory. The combination of internal and external associations promotes meaningful learning and memory.

IMPLICATIONS FOR BUILDING ASSOCIATIONS

This section provides specific implications for how teachers can help students build internal and external associations.

Raise Association Questions

Instructors can raise a variety of questions geared toward association. Here is a partial list of powerful association questions.

What's above, below, and alongside?

Suppose you are teaching students about triangles. You can help build associations by raising the "what's above, below, and alongside" question. Students then learn these important associations: Triangles have subtypes (equilateral, isosceles, and scalene—what's below?); triangles are a type of geometric shape (what's above?); and triangles are geometric shapes just like squares and rectangles (what's alongside?). These three questions are always appropriate when information is organized hierarchically. Remember the bird hierarchy in Chapter 3 (Exhibit 3.12)? When learning about swans, we can ask what's above (water birds), what's below (trumpeter and black), and what's alongside (raptors and song birds). When information is organized sequentially, then the "what's alongside" question is most appropriate and can be rephrased: "What's before and after?" For instance, when learning that food is partially digested in the stomach, ask what happens to the food before and after entering the stomach. Similarly, when learning about the Battle of Gettysburg, ask about the events preceding and following the battle.

How are these things alike and different?

Whenever learning about two or more things ask students how they are alike and different. The things must be alike because they are presented collectively; they must be different because they each have a unique name. For example, when learning about atriums and ventricles, ask how they are alike (both are parts of the heart) and how they are different (the atriums are the soft-walled upper chambers, and the ventricles are the tough-walled lower chambers). When learning about proactive and retroactive interference in psychology, ask how they are alike—both are forms of forgetting where the learning of one stimulus blocks the recall of a second stimulus—and different—the interfering stimulus either comes before (proactive) or after (retroactive) the stimulus to be recalled.

What's the association between structure and function?

In science, all things have a structure and function. In every case there is some association between the two. For example, let's revisit the atriums and ventricles mentioned just above where we learned their structures: Atriums are soft walled and ventricles are tough walled. Their functions are related to their structures. Atriums are soft walled because they passively receive blood. Ventricles are tough walled because they are composed of muscle needed to pump blood throughout the body. Another example: Incisor teeth are pointed (structure) to tear food (function), whereas molar teeth are large and flat (structure) to grind food (function).

What common categories cut across the topics?

Whenever two or more topics are presented, ask students to identify the set of common categories along which the topics can be compared. For example, when learning about different cloud formations (such as cumulus, stratus, and cirrus) ask what categories cut across cloud formations. Students soon realize that all cloud types must have an appearance, composition, elevation, and weather patterns. When this information is uncovered, students are likely to make associations among clouds like the following: Cumulus and cirrus clouds are white, whereas stratus clouds are gray; stratus clouds are low, cirrus clouds are high, and cumulus clouds are at varying altitudes; stratus and cumulus clouds are associated with precipitation, whereas cirrus clouds are associated with fair weather. Here are some other topics and potential common categories.

(Continued)

(Continued)

> Wars—parties involved, location, cause, outcome, time
> Stories—plot, characters, setting, author, genre
> Paintings—title, period, artist, subject, style
> Cell Parts—structure, function, location

What do I know about this?

Learning depends on new information being associated with previously acquired information. This external association helps learners understand and remember new information. For example, when students learn Native Americans living in the Pacific Northwest built homes made of wood planks with slanted roofs, help them associate these seemingly arbitrary ideas with meaningful prior knowledge. Students probably know that the Pacific Northwest has a lot of rain and many large trees. The abundance of rain explains the slanted roofs, and the many large trees explain the wood planks. By associating the new information to prior knowledge, the new information is now meaningful and easily remembered. Here is another example. When learning about the economic law of supply and demand students can be encouraged to associate the law with personal experiences. I for one might associate the law to my experience waiting in lines for up to an hour to buy gas during the gas shortage of the 1970s. When gas supplies were short, demand was high.

Why?

The "why" question is a variation of the "what do I know about this" question (Pressley, Symons, McDaniel, Snyder, & Turnure, 1988.) In each case, prior knowledge is associated with the information learned. The "why" question is more specific, though, because the resulting association is always a meaningful explanation for the information learned. As an example, read the passage about animal learning presented in Exhibit 4.5 and then examine the possible questions and explanations a teacher might raise below.

EXHIBIT 4.5   Animal Learning Passage

Animal Behavior

The study of animal behavior is approached in contrasting ways by two types of psychologists: comparative psychologists and ethologists.

Comparative psychologists can be compared with ethologists along several dimensions. Comparative psychologists study animal behavior in laboratory settings. They conduct diligent experiments on a few animal species, trying to uncover general learning principles common to all animals. These American psychologists believe that behavior is learned.

Ethologists, on the other hand, study animal behavior in the animal's natural surroundings. Their methods are less rigorous. They usually observe animals. Ethologists study many animals to learn how each behaves. These European psychologists believe that behavior is innate.

1. *Why* study animals in laboratories? The animals are easier to control and observe.

2. *Why* do comparative psychologists believe behavior is learned? Their studies show that animals are capable of learning new behaviors such as pressing a lever for food.

3. *Why* study behavior in the animal's natural surrounding? Probably, to see how it behaves in the real world. You can't see how a hawk really hunts, for example, in a laboratory.

4. *Why* do ethologists believe behavior is innate? They must see that various animals do things instinctively such as building a nest without training.

Use Representations to Build Associations

Representations are constructed for the purpose of building associations. When constructed properly, representations reveal the intended message almost at once. Therefore, teachers and students should study representations looking for within-topic and across-topic internal associations and external associations. Each association type is described and exemplified relative to the comprehensive wildcat matrix presented in Exhibit 4.6. A scaled-down version appeared in Chapter 3.

Within-topic associations are those made within a single topic. For instance, looking down the tiger topic in Exhibit 4.6, the tiger's powerful upper body can be associated with its hunting method of knocking over prey. Another within-topic, association is found within the cheetah topic. Note that the cheetah's powerful, athletic legs are well suited for running down its prey.

Across-topic associations are those made within one or more categories. Below are associations made across a single category:

- Wildcats range in weight from 30 to 450 pounds.
- Tigers and lions roar.
- Wildcat ranges range from five to 150 square miles.

Below are sample across-topic associations made across two or more categories. These more global associations are especially effective in revealing the intended message or the big picture:

- Big cats roar; medium-sized cats growl; small cats purr.
- Cats with keen eyes and ears stalk their prey.
- Jungle cats are solitary; plains cats live in groups.

| **EXHIBIT 4.6** | Wildcat Matrix | | | | | |

	Tiger	Lion	Jaguar	Leopard	Cheetah	Bobcat
Physical features						
Call:	Roar	Roar	Growl	Growl	Purr	Purr
Maximum weight (lb):	450	400	200	150	125	30
Distinctive characteristics:	Powerful upper body	Powerful upper body	Keen eyes and ears	Tremendous strength, keen eyes and ears	Powerful athletic legs	Keen eyes and ears
Lifestyle						
Habitat:	Jungle	Plains	Jungle	Jungle	Plains	Jungle
Range (sq. miles):	30	150	5	15	50	30
Social behavior:	Solitary	Groups	Solitary	Solitary	Groups	Solitary
Hunting method	Knocks prey over	Knocks prey over	Stalks prey	Stalks prey	Runs down prey	Stalks prey

External associations. External associations, as you know, are those that extend beyond the information given. A teacher might point out that the tiger is like a linebacker because it has a big upper body and tackles its prey or that the cheetah is like a sprinter because it is fast and has powerful legs.

Anchor Instruction

Too often, information is taught and learned in ways that render it virtually meaningless and unusable. When I was a graduate student, I took a statistics course in multivariate analysis and earned a perfect score on the final exam. Unfortunately, my perceived statistical wizardry was short lived. Just days later, I met with my adviser and discussed plans for analyzing data from a study we conducted. Our conversation revealed that I could not identify the appropriate test—a multivariate analysis—or carry out the analysis. Somehow, I had aced the exam but failed to acquire useful knowledge. How did that happen? It happened because the statistical ideas were never anchored to meaningful ideas or experiences. The learning of statistical formula, the scientific method, and the functions of cell parts all depend on anchoring new learning to meaningful ideas or experiences.

Psychologist John Bransford (Cognition and Technology Group at Vanderbilt, 1997) developed several instructional units based on anchored instruction. In one unit, elementary students learn about the scientific method in the context of an animated story. The story, *Rabbit and the Magic Hats*, involves Rabbit and other characters living on a tiny planet who are visited by a stranger named Wongo. Wongo tells the animals that they need to buy his "magic" hats to improve their imaginations and tell good stories. All the animals are deceived by his pitch except for Rabbit who uses the scientific method to test whether the hats are really magic. Rabbit's tests confirm that the hats are powerless. In this example, learning about the scientific method is anchored to a meaningful and memorable context—*Rabbit and the Magic Hats.* The story anchor is the means for learning and later retrieving useful knowledge.

Another example of anchored instruction pertains to cell part functions. This new information can be anchored to already familiar information about parts of a city and their comparable functions. For example, a cell wall can be anchored to the wall that surrounds a city. In both cases the wall defines the boundary and protects against intruders. The cell membrane can be anchored to the border guards within a city. Both allow good material in and keep harmful material out. The mitochondria can be anchored to the city library because both function as information centers.

Provide Examples

Do you know when to use a comma versus a semicolon? It's easy. Here are the rules: Use a comma when two main clauses are joined by a coordinate conjunction; use a semicolon when two main clauses are not joined by a coordinate conjunction. Got that? Probably not; you're probably unsure what is meant by main clause and coordinate conjunction. Although you could no doubt memorize these grammar rules, it's unlikely you could apply them. What would help are examples. "Sticks and stones can break my bones, but names can never hurt me" is an example of proper comma usage for joining main clauses with a coordinate conjunction. Alternatively, "Sticks and stones can break my bones; names can never hurt me" is an example of proper semicolon usage for joining main clauses without a coordinate conjunction. By associating these examples with their rules, we see that main clauses are parts of sentences that can stand like independent sentences (i.e., Sticks and stones can break my bones. Names can never hurt me.) and that coordinate conjunctions are joining words such as *but*, *and*, *so*, and *or*. In sum, we learn that two main clauses joined by a coordinate conjunction include a comma; two main clauses not joined by a coordinate conjunction include a semicolon. More important, we see that learning depends on associating examples with their referent.

Exhibit 4.7 displays a representation showing the definition and several examples of positive reinforcement. There are three important things to grasp from this exhibit. The first is that associations are made between *parts* of definitions and corresponding *parts* of examples (Atkinson, Derry, Renkl, & Wortham, 2000). In this case, the definition for positive reinforcement contains three parts. Each part is matched with the corresponding example part. Students must learn that the dog performing a trick is an example of behavior, the dog being fed is an example of a presented stimulus, and the dog performing the trick more often is an example of increased behavior. In order to fully understand a definition and its parts, the association between definition parts and example parts must be made.

The second important thing to grasp from Exhibit 4.7 is the importance of presenting a range of examples (Tennyson & Cocchiarella, 1986). Notice that three examples are presented and that the examples are quite varied. By presenting a range of examples, students more fully learn the concept of positive reinforcement. They learn (a) that positive reinforcement can apply to positive behaviors such as tricks or studying or to negative behaviors such as howling, (b) that presented stimuli can seem favorable such as receiving a food treat or high grade or seem aversive such as being yelled at, and (c) that the context can pertain to animal or human learning. Creating associations among the range of examples helps learners deduce that positive reinforcement occurs whenever any presented stimulus works to increase any behavior. Had just one example been presented, students would later be unable to recognize many varied examples of positive reinforcement.

Children exposed to a single dog, such as a dachshund, might be unable to recognize other dogs, especially big furry ones, and a physician shown limited examples of a disease might have trouble diagnosing that disease. My friend, Tom, is a doctor. When he was about 35 years old he developed a rash on his chest. He was unsure what it was, so he did something that no doctor ever wants to do: play golf on a public course. No, that wasn't it; he made an appointment and went to see another doctor as if he was a mere mortal. Just like you and me, Tom waited for hours in a crowded waiting room before finally being called back to the examining room where he had to wait another 45 minutes on cold butcher block

EXHIBIT 4.7   Definition and Examples of Positive Reinforcement

Positive Reinforcement				
Definition:	Behavior	→	Presented Stimulus	→	Increased Behavior
Example 1:	Dog trick		Feed dog		Trick preformed more often
Example 2:	Dog howling		Yell at dog		Howling increases
Example 3:	Student studies		Receives high grade		Studies more often
Nonexample 1:	Dog trick		Feed dog		Dog stops doing trick
Nonexample 2:	Student studies		Remove detention		Studies more often

paper wearing a backless, bottomless gown. When the doctor, a specialist in dermatology, finally arrived, he diagnosed Tom's rash in an eye-blink—shingles . . . $230.00, please. How did Tom miss the costly diagnosis? Here's how: When he learned about shingles, he saw just classic examples—namely, acute, painful cases among the elderly where it is most common. He did not experience a range of examples such as mild cases among the young and healthy.

The third important point to grasp from Exhibit 4.7 is nonexamples facilitate learning too (Joyce, Weil, &Calhoun, 2000). Whereas examples help learners generalize their knowledge to a wide range of settings, nonexamples help learners discriminate what they are learning from other things. In the case of positive reinforcement, wide ranging examples show the breadth of positive reinforcement, whereas nonexamples show its limits. The first nonexample shows that even though a positive stimulus (food) was presented, positive reinforcement did not occur because the behavior (the dog trick) did not occur again. The second nonexample shows that even though the behavior of studying increased, positive reinforcement did not occur because the stimulus of detention was removed rather than presented.

EXHIBIT 4.8   Example Circle

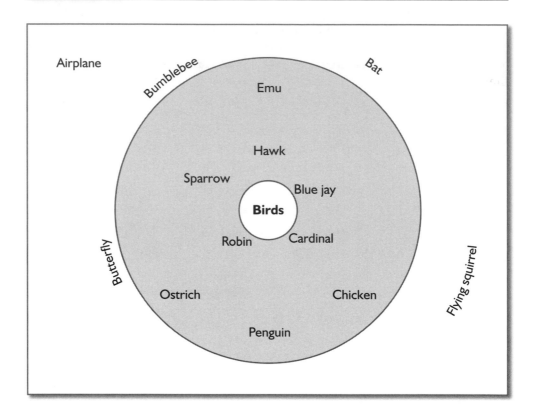

When presenting students with a range of examples and nonexamples, you might help students construct an example circle like that in Exhibit 4.8. The central concept, in this case "birds," is placed in the circle's center. Inside the circle is a range of birds examples with the more typical or classic birds, such as robins and blue jays, toward the center and the less typical birds, such as emus, ostriches, and penguins, toward the inner boundary. The range of examples helps students generalize the bird concept so they can recognize any bird. Outside the circle is a range of nonexamples with the obvious nonexamples, such as airplane and flying squirrel, appearing furthest from the circle boundary and the not as obvious nonexamples, such as bat and bumblebee, appearing closest to the circle's outer boundary. The nonexamples help learners discriminate birds from other things.

Provide Mnemonics

Sometimes students lack the meaningful background knowledge necessary to construct external associations. If they simply do not know there is an abundance of timber and heavy rains in the Pacific Northwest, then they cannot use this knowledge to understand why Native American homes built there had slanted roofs (to increase water run off from heavy rains) made from wood planks (because of the abundance of timber). When meaningful associations cannot be made, then contrived associations are the next best bet. In this case, a learner might visualize a map of the United States with a wooden plank in the Pacific Northwest slanting down into the Pacific Ocean like a water slide. This image reminds the learner that homes in that region were built with slanted wood roofs. Contrived associations intended to improve memory are called mnemonics. There are five main types of mnemonic devices that can help students remember information.

First-Letter

In this system, the first letter of each to-be-learned term is used to form a new word or sentence. There are many popular examples.

- **Roy G. Biv** is used to remember the order of colors in a rainbow: **r**ed, **o**range, **y**ellow, **g**reen, **b**lue, **i**ndigo, and **v**iolet. Teaching this popular mnemonic has long been a national requirement in schools. If you somehow missed learning this, please contact me. I am forming a class-action suit on your behalf.

- **M**y **v**ery **e**ducated **m**other **j**ust **s**erved **us** **n**achos. The first letters in this sentence represent the first letters of planets in our solar system extending outward from the sun: **M**ercury, **V**enus, **E**arth, **M**ars, **J**upiter, **S**aturn, **U**ranus, and **N**eptune . . . with apologies to Pluto.

- **HOMES** stands for the Great Lakes: **H**uron, **O**ntario, **M**ichigan, **E**rie, and **S**uperior.

- **P**lease **e**xcuse **m**y **d**ear **A**unt **S**ally provides the first letters associated with the order of operations in math: **p**arentheses, **e**xponents, **m**ultiplication, **d**ivision, **a**ddition, and **s**ubtraction.

Narrative Chaining

Narrative chaining is a mnemonic system where the to-be-learned terms (or something that sounds like them) are sewn together into a memorable story. Narrative chaining was used to remember parts of a plant's reproductive system in my junior high school science class. When the teacher first announced that we would learn the reproductive parts of plants my buddies and I were in a tizzy. Back then, there was no sex education. Our education came from the streets, where we scoured trash receptacles for discarded *National Geographic* magazines, and from the long awaited study of botany. In the weeks preceding the plant reproduction unit, the boys' room banter was pure botany. "My brother took this course two years ago and told me we cover the anther and stigma—oh, baby." One time, Ronnie Foot even smuggled a copy of *Plants and Gardens* from home and showed it around the boys' room—"Check out that style . . . hubba, hubba."

When the big day finally arrived, I remember our science teacher using what I now recognize as narrative chaining to introduce the reproductive plant parts: "*Stamen, stigma style,* or I'll shoot you with my *pistil.*" And "That's what Phil meant (*filament*) when he went *ovary* his *anther.*" No wonder I couldn't get a date in college. This same teacher, by the way, helped students learn about the circulatory system using narrative chaining. He told the story of Gene Cell who drove his little red corpuscle down pulmonary vein wondering whether he aorta turn right to heartland. Who would ever remember this stuff?

Peg-Word Method

The peg-word method works great for remembering lists. And much of what is learned is a list or a list in disguise. Here are just a few listlike things learned: the process of digestion, English kings, bones in the leg, key points in a speech, and books in the Harry Potter series. To remember as many as 10 items in a list, first establish 10 visual pegs in memory—each associated with a number 1 through 10. These pegs are later used to hang the list information just as wall pegs are used to hang clothing. My own peg for number one is a bun because it rhymes with one. Continuing the rhyming theme: two is a shoe, three is a tree, and four is a door. Five is golden rings in harmony with the Christmas tune, *The 12 Days of Christmas.* Six is a six-pack. Seven is Mickey Mantle, the great Yankee player who donned number seven. Eight is a gate—revisiting the rhyming theme. Nine is a cat because a cat has nine lives, and ten is tent because it sounds like ten.

Suppose students had to learn a list of 10 healthy habits: (1) drink plenty of water, (2) get enough sleep, (3) exercise daily, (4) read, (5) be friends, (6) eat fruits, (7) eat vegetables, (8) eat grains, (9) buckle your seatbelt, and (10) wear a helmet when biking. These can be learned using the peg-word method by creating the following visual images in memory linking the pegs and list items: (1) a bun soaked in water, (2) a shoe on a pillow, (3) climbing a tree, (4) a book propping a door open, (5) friends showing off their rings, (6) a six-pack of apples, (7) Mickey Mantle batting with a carrot, (8) a gate in a wheat field, (9) a cat buckled up for a car ride, and (10) a tent stuffed with bike helmets.

These visual associations are rock solid. If asked to recall the list, a student need only revisit the pegs and the associated list words are recalled as well. Although this might seem like a difficult system to employ, it really is not. I have demonstrated it many times in class and even a few times to liven up a dying party. Who needs lampshades when you have mnemonics?

Keyword Method

The keyword method is an effective technique for teaching vocabulary, such as foreign language words or science terms (Atkinson & Raugh, 1975). It's also useful for teaching word pairs such as states and capitals, or composers and their works. Let's first see how it works for foreign language vocabulary. Suppose you were teaching that the Spanish word *trigo* means wheat. Here's what to do:

1. Create a keyword by associating *trigo* with a familiar English word or phrase (the keyword) that sounds like *trigo*—perhaps *tree*.

2. Create an image linking the keyword (tree) to the word's meaning (wheat). For example, imagine a wheat tree.

That image helps you remember that *trigo* means wheat. Exhibit 4.9 is a representation showing the keyword method.

Try using the keyword method to learn that the German word *tannenbaum* means Christmas tree. First, create a keyword—*tannenbaum* sounds like *tied and bound*. Next, create an image of a Christmas tree that is tied and

EXHIBIT 4.9 Keyword Method

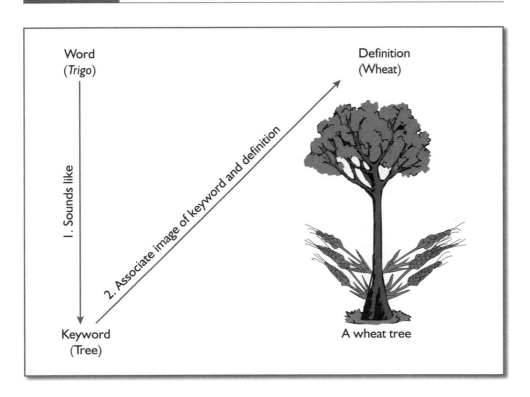

bound to a car roof. This image helps you remember that *tannenbaum* means Christmas tree.

The keyword method works just as well for learning English vocabulary. Here are two examples:

- Fob is a short chain. *Fob* sounds like *lob*. Imagine a tennis player hitting a lob with a short chain dangling from the ball.
- Lyceum is a concert hall. *Lyceum* sounds like *lice*. Imagine musicians in a concert hall unable to play because they are scratching lice in their heads.

The following are examples of how the keyword method can be used for learning scientific information about the location of bones.

- Scapula is the shoulder blade. *Scapula* sounds like *spatula*. Imagine a spatula scraping something off your shoulder.
- Carpals are wrist bones. *Carpals* sound like *car pals*. Imagine pals in a car handcuffed at the wrist.

To learn states and capitals, first create two keywords—one for the capital and one for the state. Second, create an image associating these keywords. Let's try Topeka, Kansas. *Topeka* sounds like *toe* and *peek*. *Kansas* sounds like *can*. Imagine a toe peeking from a can as shown in Exhibit 4.10. Finally, let's use the keyword method to associate composers and their compositions. Tchaikovsky composed *Swan Lake*. *Tchaikovsky* sounds like *cough ski*. Imagine a woman coughing as she skis across a lake filled with swans.

Mnemonomy

A mnemonomy is a pictorial representation that helps learners associate and remember several facts (Atkinson et al., 1999; Carney & Levin, 2000). For example, suppose students were to learn that tigers roar, weigh 450 pounds, have powerful upper bodies, and are solitary. The mnemonomy in Exhibit 4.11 combines all those facts within a single illustration. Note that the tiger is on a scale showing its weight (450 pounds), is flexing its powerful upper body, is roaring its approval, and is alone (solitary). The mnemonomy in Exhibit 4.12 helps students learn that black rhinos live in the jungles of southern Africa, have two horns, are solitary, act aggressively, and eat twigs, which they grasp with hooked lips.

Mnemonics are powerful and fun to use. Realize though, mnemonics hold a small but important place in teaching and learning. They should be used sparingly to remember bits of information that cannot be more meaningfully learned. For example, only after constructing a matrix comparing moths and butterflies and building meaningful associations, such as

EXHIBIT 4.10   Keyword Method for Learning States and Capitals

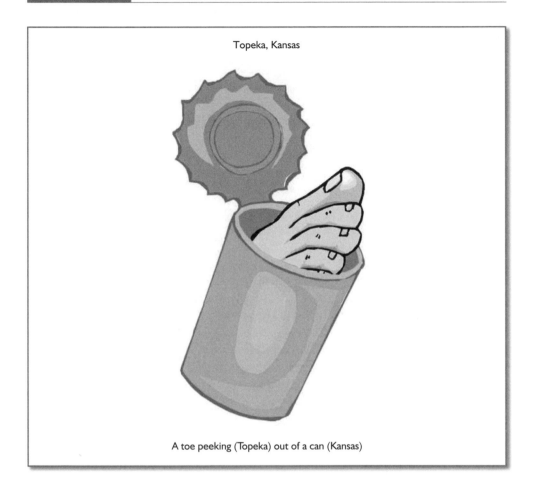

Topeka, Kansas

A toe peeking (Topeka) out of a can (Kansas)

"butterflies have more vibrant characteristics than moths," should mnemonics be used to clean up any details. At that point, the keyword method might be used to remember that the unfamiliar word *pupa* (sounds like pupil) means cocoon by imagining an eye peering out from a cocoon.

STRATEGY INSTRUCTION: TEACHING STUDENTS TO ASSOCIATE

Instructors can easily embed strategy training for creating associations in their class. Below are excerpts of what an instructor might say while teaching students about fish and concurrently teaching the "why" association strategy.

EXHIBIT 4.11   A Mnemonomy for Remembering Tiger Facts

The *tiger* is on a scale showing its *weight* (450 pounds), is flexing its *powerful upper body, is roaring* its approval, and is *alone* (solitary).

"The text indicates that crappies have a mottled appearance and live in the rocks or along the bottom, whereas croaker fish have vertical stripes and live among vegetation. Perhaps, you could simply memorize this information but you could easily forget it or confuse it because it seems arbitrary. Let me teach you a strategy called 'why questions' (*Introduce the strategy*) that helps you associate and better understand information." (*Sell the strategy*)

"When learning information that seems arbitrary raise the 'why' question. Ask and answer as best you can why something is

EXHIBIT 4.12   A Mnemonomy for Remembering Black Rhino Facts

The solitary black rhino from the jungle of southern Africa
is aggressive, has two horns, and hooked lips for eating twigs.

so. In the case of fish, I wonder why the crappie has a mottled appearance and how its appearance might relate to its habitat. I know from past experience that many animals, such as deer and polar bears, blend into their surroundings so they won't easily be detected by predators or prey. Perhaps, the crappie has a mottled appearance suited for hiding among rocks or at a lake's darkened bottom. Similarly, I ask why the croaker has vertical stripes and reason that its stripes allow it to hide among vegetation." (*Introduce the strategy*)

"Now try using the 'why' strategy to learn about the other two fish presented in your text. Question and explain the relationship between the catfish's appearance and habitat and the albacore's appearance and habitat. Later, we'll also use the 'why' strategy when learning about the location of glands relative to their functions." (*Perfect and generalize the strategy*)

5

Helping Students Regulate

To SOAR to success, students must select, organize, and associate information. They must also regulate by monitoring and assessing learning along the way. With good regulation students know if they know . . . before a teacher tests them. This chapter introduces regulation and then details how teachers can boost students' regulation before, during, and after instruction. As with previous chapters, it also demonstrates how teachers can teach students how to regulate on their own.

INTRODUCING REGULATION

If you had a crystal ball perhaps you could see the future. Gazing into the cloudy, glass ball one morning, you might foresee your principal stopping by and observing your class later today and things going miserably because your lesson is not well planned, and you might foresee a minor traffic accident this evening when you back your SUV into a car in a grocery store parking lot. Better go back to bed.

Well, you do have a crystal ball, of sorts, that can foretell the future: Its name is *regulation*. Successful people regulate their lives. They think about what the future might hold and take steps to control it. A regulator knows that the principal drops by classrooms unexpectedly and observes teachers several times a year. Knowing this, the teacher's lessons are always well prepared. Or the teacher at least preserves a few can't miss lessons in the desk drawer for such occasions. As for the traffic accident, a regulator knows that a busy, dark parking lot is a breeding ground for fender benders, especially when you drive a big SUV with limited sight lines. Knowing this, the driver parks in a remote corner of the lot, keeps the mirrors and windows clean, and only creeps backward after checking all mirrors and turning to look.

You've seen that regulation helps you look ahead, but it also helps you look around and look back. You can regulate the future, present, and past. As for the present, read the passage below:

> The man was worried. His car came to a halt and he was all alone. It was extremely dark and cold. The man took off his overcoat, rolled down the window, and got out of the car as quickly as possible. Then he used all his strength to move as fast as he could. He was relieved when he saw the lights of the city, even though they were far away. (Bransford, 1979, p. 151)

Did you understand the passage? Most people say they understood it; after all, there were no new vocabulary words and it was short and easy to read. But did you really understand it? If so, you would be able to answer the following questions: Why did the man take off his overcoat if it was cold? Why did he roll down his window? Why did he have to use all of his strength to move? Why was he relieved to see the city lights?

Exposed to these questions, you finally understand that you don't understand; you finally know that you don't know. The questions posed helped you regulate your learning and determine that comprehension was poor. Of course, good regulators do not wait for someone else to pose questions; good regulators do so independently while reading the passage. In the present moment, regulators assess comprehension and know whether or not they know. The passage, by the way, was about a car submerged in an icy lake.

Good regulators regulate all aspects of their present lives. Teachers presenting a lesson ask, "Is my lesson clear; do students understand?" Coaches ask, "Is this defense working; should we switch to a different formation?" Drivers regulate by checking speed, following distance, and adjacent lane traffic. Golfers regulate club selection, grip, stance, and swing. And writers monitor message clarity, grammar, punctuation, and spelling. The better we regulate—the more in tune we are with what's happening—the better we perform.

Regulation's work does not end with the closing school bell, the game's final whistle, a counterclockwise turn of the ignition key, a strike of the golf ball, or when the last sentence is composed. Regulation is also for looking back and assessing what went right and, especially, what went wrong. Everyone makes mistakes—even the great ones. But with failure comes opportunity to regulate what went wrong and how to improve it. Consider how the regulation of mistakes finally got the Wright brothers airborne. The Wright brothers' success was built on failures, a lot of them. Over nearly 10 years, the brothers built and rebuilt seven planes, having crashed every one of them more than once. It took them over 200 tries alone to perfect the eventual wing shape. Regulating past mistakes helped them soar. And students cannot soar without regulation—the "R" in SOAR. Teachers who help students regulate future, present, and past learning help students soar to success.

AIDING REGULATION BEFORE LEARNING

I have an assignment for you: Give me financial advice; submit your recommendations in one week. This vague assignment probably leaves you scratching your head. You wonder, "What kind of financial advice?" Should you prepare advice about individual retirement accounts, college savings plans, prepaying a mortgage, eligible tax deductions, or balancing a checkbook? You just don't know. You cannot regulate your progress toward meeting this assignment because you really don't understand the assignment. You're left spinning your wheels.

Students are often faced with "give me financial advice" type guidance or assignments. Teachers are sometimes vague or secretive about what students should do or learn even though students need this information to move forward. A teacher who says "your test will cover the skeletal system" provides minimal guidance. Students do not know whether they have to name the bones, draw them, recognize them on a skeleton, or know their composition and functions? Students are unsure how or what to study. A teacher who assigns students to "write a paper about George Washington" leaves students unclear about the focus of the paper (his youth, military experience, political career, or legacy) and how it will be assessed (accuracy, organization, length, interest, or sentence structure).

Why do teachers shroud the criteria in secrecy? Two reasons come to mind. First, teachers might not be sure just how students will be assessed. Some might not think about assessment until they write the test the night before or until it's time to grade papers and projects. Second, some teachers believe that students should figure out for themselves what will be tested or what constitutes an "A" paper. After all, when teachers were students, their teachers withheld such information as if it were a military secret.

For maximal learning to occur, teachers must establish how students' performance will be assessed and inform students about expected performance prior to learning. With a clear goal in mind, students know what they must accomplish and can regulate progress toward the goal. Three proven methods for guiding students before learning begins are objectives, grading rubrics, and timelines. Each is described in turn.

Objectives

Objectives convey intended learning outcomes. They specify what students will be able to do following instruction. Let me emphasize that objectives are not about what teachers do during instruction; they are about what students must do following instruction. "I will teach you a clever way to memorize the names of the bones" and "I will compare Washington to contemporary presidents" are not examples of objectives. Both specify teacher behaviors, not learning outcomes. An objective might inform students that they "need to label bones on a skeletal x-ray" or "compare Washington's foreign policy with that of our current president."

Objectives specify three things: the assessment *conditions,* the demonstrated *behavior,* and the *standards* for judging performance (Dick, Carey, & Carey, 2005, chap. 6). Objectives describe the conditions under which behavior occurs when assessed. Suppose the intended behavior is free-throw shooting in basketball. When assessing this behavior, the coach might have the player shoot 10 consecutive free throws in a quiet gym. Alternatively, the coach might have the player run a sprint just before each free throw and have others nearby wave and scream as each shot is attempted. You'll agree that these are drastically different conditions for free-throw shooting and that a player would want to know the assessment conditions in advance in order to practice and regulate performance accordingly.

Objectives specify the behavior performed. The behavior is something observable and measurable. An objective would never state that a player must "understand free-throw shooting" because we cannot see or gauge understanding. We can, however, observe and gauge the behavior of "shooting free throws."

Standards specify the acceptable level of performance. The player attempting 10 free throws might need to sink a minimum of 7 to meet the objective. That's a quantitative standard. Standards can also set the expected behavior quality. Acceptable free throws might be those shot with "correct release and follow through."

When expressing objectives, it is usually convenient to specify the conditions, behavior, and standards in that order. Below are three sample mathematical objectives expressed in that fashion:

1. Upon request (condition), the student will list the three characteristics of right triangles (behavior), without error (standard).

2. Given a number of geometric shapes (condition), the student will circle just the right triangles (behavior), with 80% accuracy (standard).

3. Given a number of right triangles with the length of two sides marked (condition), the student will calculate and write the correct length of the unknown side (behavior), for at least 80% of the problems (standard).

Look how helpful these objectives are to both teacher and student. The teacher knows exactly what must be taught and can plan accordingly; the student knows exactly what must be learned and can learn accordingly. The teacher can easily generate test items that correspond to objectives—and so can students. A corresponding item appears below relative to each objective.

1. List the three characteristics of right triangles.

2. Below are four geometric shapes. Circle only the right triangles.

3. Calculate the length of the unmarked side for each of the following right triangles.

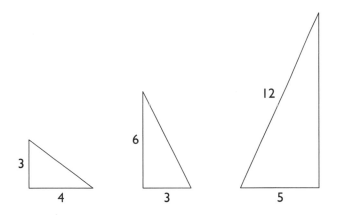

Some critics argue that providing students with objectives is paramount to telling students the test questions in advance. That criticism is largely false. Consider that there is an infinite number of ways to test Objective 2 by providing various right triangles and non-right triangles and Objective 3 by providing various length calculation problems. Objective 1 is more limited in how it can be assessed, but so what? If you want students to learn the characteristics of right triangles, why not tell them? Critics also argue that objectives limit learning: Students learn information pertaining to objectives but overlook information not pertaining to objectives. That's true, but not a problem. If you want students to learn information outside the objectives, simply provide objectives pertaining to that "outside" information. Critics need to understand that students given objectives learn the objective-related information better than students not given objectives (see Dick et al., 2005, p. 124).

You've seen that objectives specify the conditions, behavior, and standards. They specify one more important thing: the type of learning outcome (Gagne, 1985, chap. 3). Take another look at Objectives 1–3 above. Each pertains to a different type of learning. Objective 1 pertains to *fact* learning. Students need to learn three facts associated with right triangles: They are closed, three sided, and contain a 90° angle. Objective 2 pertains to *concept* learning. Students need to recognize new examples of the concept "right triangle" from nonexamples. Objective 3 pertains to *skill* learning. Students need to demonstrate the skill of calculating the length of a right triangle's unmarked side using Pythagoras's theorem: $C^2 = A^2 + B^2$.

To help you recognize different learning outcomes, here are three more objectives from the literature domain that reflect fact, concept, and skill learning, respectively.

1. Upon request, the student will list the characteristics of a haiku poem, without error.

2. Given a number of previously unread poems, the student will mark the haikus, with 90% accuracy.

3. Given a novel topic, the student will compose a haiku about that topic, which fulfills the criteria for haikus (three unrhymed lines with 5, 7, and 5 syllables, respectively).

Notice that Objective 1 requires fact learning—the *knowing* of information, Objective 2 requires concept learning—the *recognition* of new examples, and Objective 3 requires skill learning—the *showing* of knowledge. Even though the objectives pertain to the same topic, what students must learn and do to meet each objective varies widely. More is said about fact, concept, and skill learning later in the "During Learning" section of this chapter.

Grading Rubrics

A grading rubric shows the criteria used for grading an assignment. For instance, the criteria for grading an English assignment might be organization, information, and mechanics as shown in the leftmost column of Exhibit 5.1. Each criterion is then divided into evaluation levels such as 1 through 4. In Exhibit 5.1, Level 4 represents high achievement and Level 1 represents low achievement. A description of expected performance is provided for each criterion at each level. For instance, the rubric in Exhibit 5.1 designates what is needed to attain a score of 1, 2, 3, or 4 for organization along the middle row. A grading rubric makes clear at the outset what

EXHIBIT 5.1   Grading Rubric for an English Assignment

Category	4	3	2	1
Information	All topics addressed fully; complete supporting information	All topics addressed; some supporting information	Most topics addressed; minimal supporting information	Multiple topics not addressed; little or no supporting information
Organization	Ideas well organized; excellent use of paragraphs, headings, and subheadings	Ideas well organized; good use of paragraphs; some headings and subheadings	Ideas well organized; fair paragraph structure; few headings and subheadings	Disorganized information with weak paragraph structure
Mechanics	No errors	1–5 errors	6–10 errors	More than 10 errors

students must do to achieve a certain score and how teachers will grade the assignment. Certain Web sites assist teachers in developing grading rubrics.

Exhibit 5.2 shows another grading rubric used to guide and judge instrumental music performance. The criteria listed down the leftmost column are tone quality, rhythm, and expression and style. The performance levels for each criterion shown across the top row are the standard grades A, B, C, and D. A student receiving this grading rubric knows the expected performance for each criterion in advance and can regulate learning accordingly.

Timelines

A timeline designates an assignment's subtasks and when each subtask should be completed. For example, suppose students are assigned to write a paper about one aspect of George Washington's life. The timeline in Exhibit 5.3 shows the paper's due date, various subtasks for completing the paper (choose topic, review literature, represent paper's structure, compose first draft, compose second draft, and complete final draft), and the respective date for completing each subtask. Even if students need only turn in the final paper, the timeline helps them regulate their progress toward completion.

EXHIBIT 5.2   Grading Rubric for Instrumental Music Performance

Category	A	B	C
Tone	Consistently full and sustained throughout range	Usually full and sustained in normal range but is limited and warbles in extreme range	Uncontrolled regardless of range
Rhythm	Accurate	Usually accurate but some duration errors	Erratic with frequent duration errors
Expression	Captures the intended mood	Somewhat expressive and usually in line with intended mood	General lack of expression

EXHIBIT 5.3   Timeline for Completing a Paper

Task:	Choose Topic	→ Review Literature	→ Represent Paper's Structure	→ Compose First Draft	→ Compose Second Draft	→ Compose Final Draft
Due date:	September 4	September 18	October 1	October 15	October 30	November 15

A timeline can also be given to students who must complete a large reading assignment. Too often, students wait too long to begin reading or read too little and fall behind. A timeline helps students keep and regulate pace. A simple timeline like that in Exhibit 5.4 provides a plan for smoothly completing a large reading assignment.

AIDING REGULATION DURING LEARNING

Objectives and scoring rubrics are helpful because they tell students about the expected performance and how it will be judged. Armed with this knowledge, students know what they must do and can regulate their progress. Still, knowing what must be done falls short of actually doing it. That's why, during instruction, instructors should provide practice tests

EXHIBIT 5.4	Timeline for Completing a Reading Assignment

Chapter	1 →	2 →	3 →	4 →	5 →	6
Completion date	1/10	1/17	1/24	1/31	2/7	2/14

that help students practice the expected behavior (Bransford, 1979, pp. 238–244; King 1989, 1992). It is important that practice tests (and final tests) match objectives in terms of expected behavior (Dick et al., 2005). If an objective states that a student must *write the definition of an isosceles triangle,* it is unfair if the test assesses the student's ability to *recognize isosceles triangles* among other triangles. The objective calls for fact learning; the test measures concept learning. Similarly, it is unfair if the objective states that a student must *write the formula for calculating the area of a triangle* but the test assesses the student's ability to *calculate the area of a triangle.* The objective calls for fact learning; the test measures skill learning. The remainder of this section revisits the three learning outcomes—facts, concepts, and skills—in more detail and offers guidelines for writing good practice or final test items for each outcome.

When teachers tell students what kind of test to expect, they often report that the test is short answer, fill-in-the-blank, true/false, or multiple choice. That sort of test form information is only somewhat helpful. Although it helps students to know whether they need to recognize or recall information, what they really need to know is whether the test measures fact, concept, or skill learning. To see why, look at the following test questions:

1. What is the medical name for the shinbone? (short answer)

2. The medical name for the shinbone is _____. (fill-in-the-blank)

3. The tibia is the medical name for the shinbone. T or F (true/false)

4. Which is the medical name for the shinbone? (multiple choice)
   a. radius
   b. fibula
   c. femur
   d. tibia

As you can see, there is little difference among the questions. Even though the four questions differ in form, they all test exactly the same thing: the fact that the medical name for shinbone is tibia. Knowing that a test is going to be multiple choice, matching, or true/false tells students little. For example, examine the three multiple-choice questions below. Although they share the same multiple-choice form, they are as different as the Three Musketeers (even though they all wore those hats with the funny mouse ears).

1. What is the formula for finding the area of a triangle?

   a. length × width
   b. base × height
   c. one-half base × height

2. What shaded portion shows the area of a triangle?

3. What is the area of the triangle below?

   a. 15
   b. 30
   c. 11

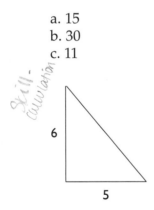

Although all three questions are in multiple-choice form, they clearly test different things. Question 1 tests a fact, knowledge of the area formula. Question 2 tests a concept, recognition of a triangle's area. Question 3 tests a skill, calculation of a triangle's area. To excel, students need to know the types of test questions to expect (fact, concept, and skill) and practice accordingly.

Are fact, concept, and skill knowledge—and their corresponding questions—really that different? They sure are. You might, for example, be able to state the definition of a *denominator* (fact) but be unable to recognize the denominator in a fraction (concept) or find the least common denominator for two fractions, such as one third and two fourths (skill). And you would certainly hope your physician can do more than name the causes of conjunctivitis (fact). Hopefully, your physician can recognize it (concept) and treat it (skill) if you were to contract the disease.

Regulate Fact Learning

Help students regulate their readiness for fact tests by providing practice items that tap the same important facts tested later. There are two main types of fact questions: single fact and relational fact. Take a look at Exhibit 5.5 showing metric units for capacity and mass. Below are single fact questions from that material.

- What is the metric capacity unit for 10?
- What is the metric mass unit for one thousandth?

Relational fact questions require students to know related facts—how two or more things compare or contrast. Here are two related fact items pertaining to metric units.

- What prefix is used for expressing a capacity or weight of 100?
- What is the metric unit for all weight measurements?

EXHIBIT 5.5   Metric Units for Capacity and Mass

	Metric Units					
	0.001	0.01	0.1	1	10	100
Capacity	Milliliter	Centiliter	Deciliter	Liter	Dekaliter	Hectoliter
Mass	Milligram	Centigram	Decigram	Gram	Dekagram	Hectogram

Regulate Concept Learning

Concepts are things that can be defined and have examples. *Triangle* is a concept. Its definition is "a closed three-sided figure." There are countless examples of triangles—big ones; small ones; and equilateral, scalene, isosceles, and right ones. The concept of triangle is easily tested by presenting students with several geometric figures like lines, angles, squares, rhombuses, and triangles and having them pick out the triangles. If they can do that, then they've acquired the triangle concept.

School subjects abound with concept learning. Physics students recognize force, inertia, and Newton's third law. Math students recognize prime and composite numbers; real and irrational numbers; multiples, numerators, addends, quotients, and remainders. Music students recognize notes, sharps, and flats; the sound of various wind instruments; and musical styles such as classic and Baroque. Language arts students recognize

EXHIBIT 5.6   Operant Conditioning Terms and Definitions

Positive reinforcement:	Presentation of a stimulus following a response that works to increase the response.
Negative reinforcement:	Removal of a stimulus following a response that works to increase the response.
Positive punishment:	Presentation of a stimulus following a response that works to decrease the response.
Negative punishment:	Removal of a stimulus following a response that works to decrease the response.

prepositional phrases, gerunds, and onomatopoeia. And physical education students learning tennis recognize lets, aces, and topspin.

Instructors teaching the operant conditioning terms and definitions in Exhibit 5.6 would want students to answer single fact questions such as, "What is the definition of positive reinforcement?" and relational fact questions such as, "Which operant techniques involve a decrease in behavior?" In addition, instructors would want students to answer concept questions like the following:

> Miranda refused to eat chicken cacciatore. One day Miranda's mother struck a deal with Miranda and gave her a quarter for every bite of chicken cacciatore she consumed. As a result, Miranda ate 29 bites of chicken cacciatore and pocketed a cool $7.25 as well. What operant technique did Miranda's mom use?

> Which one of the following examples involves negative punishment?
> a. Washing the car more often because you get paid for doing it.
> b. Losing 10 yards for holding in football and not holding thereafter.
> c. Eating out more often because you hate doing dishes.
> d. Cutting back on weight lifting because lifting makes you sore.

Teachers can regulate concept learning by having students answer practice concept questions in advance of the test. Good concept questions require that students recognize new examples of the concept. So follow these guidelines for generating concept items:

1. Do not test facts.

The following are fact questions because they require knowledge of previously provided facts or related facts, not the recognition of examples:

- What behavior outcome is associated with positive punishment?
- Which two operant techniques increase behavior?

Be cautious not to develop fact questions disguised as concept questions. The following item seems to present an example to be recognized, but the "example" is really nothing more than a restatement of the concept's definition:

- When Cindy talked with her friends during silent reading, Mr. Hoagland presented a stimulus that worked to decrease that behavior. This is an example of _____.

A much better item follows:

- When Cindy talked with her friends during silent reading, Mr. Hoagland glared at Cindy who then stopped talking. This is an example of _____.

2. Do not ask for examples.

Concept items require students to recognize new examples. Never ask students to provide examples. Here's why. Suppose during instruction I present the following example of positive reinforcement: "Madeline receives a high score in spelling, I award her a gold star, and she earns a high score on the next test too." On the test, I ask for an example of positive reinforcement and a student answers, "Madeline receives a high score in spelling, is awarded a gold star, and earns a high spelling score next time." Although the student example is correct, the student is simply repeating a previously supplied example. There is no evidence that the student could actually recognize a new example. Even if asked to provide a nonclass example, the same problem arises. The student might simply repeat an example from the textbook or one shared by a friend outside of school.

3. Do not include familiar examples.

It is important that students recognize new, previously unencountered examples to prove they've acquired the concept. Therefore, do not include on tests examples identical or similar to those provided during instruction. For example, if you presented the gold star spelling example for positive reinforcement seen earlier, do not test students' concept knowledge by having them "recognize" familiar examples or ones meaninglessly altered like the following:

- A student scores high in math, is awarded a gold star, and scores high on the next math test.
- A student scores high in spelling, is given a smiley face, and scores high on the next spelling test.

These cosmetic changes make it too easy to recognize "new" examples because they are so much like one previously encountered. Be sure examples are truly unique.

4. Test concepts amid related concepts.

A concept is rarely learned in isolation. The learning of positive reinforcement usually occurs amid the learning of related operant concepts like negative reinforcement, positive punishment, and negative punishment. The concept of triangle is usually acquired amid related geometric concepts like line, square, and rhombus. And capitalism is learned amid other governmental structures such as socialism and communism.

When testing concept knowledge—the ability to recognize new examples—it's best to have students recognize concepts against a backdrop of related and potentially confusing concepts. The purpose is not to trick students but to provide a realistic test. In the real world, stratus clouds must be discriminated from nimbus clouds; a leopard from a cheetah; blue grass from fescue; and red traffic lights from green and yellow ones.

Therefore, assess concept knowledge by having students discriminate among closely related concepts as in the example below.

- As long as Edgar is out of bed by 7:00, his father won't come into his room and blow reveille on the trumpet. This technique works to get Edgar up on time. What operant technique is at work?
    a. Positive reinforcement
    b. Negative reinforcement
    c. Positive punishment
    d. Negative punishment

Regulate Skill Learning

Try to divide the following words into syllables: *minnow, minor,* and *manor*. Having trouble? Confused? Dividing these and other words into syllables is actually easy when you apply basic rules of syllabication. The word *minnow* is divided this way: min/now. The rule is this: When a word contains a vowel, consonant, consonant, vowel sequence, divide the word

EXHIBIT 5.7   Procedure for Adding Mixed Fractions

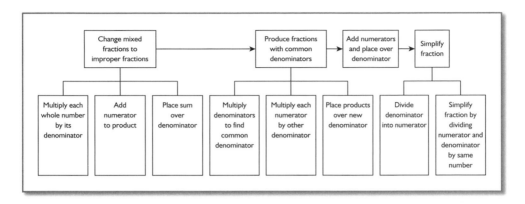

between the two consonants. The other words are divided this way: mi/nor, man/or. Here's the rule: When the vowel, consonant, vowel sequence occurs, divide the word after the first vowel if the vowel is long; if the first vowel is short, divide the word after the consonant. Knowing these rules you can easily divide words like *timber, metal,* and *toner.* Rules are one subtype of skill learning.

What is the solution to this problem: $3\frac{2}{3} + 1\frac{4}{8} = ?$ The solution is $5\frac{1}{6}$. Finding the solution requires the application of the procedure shown in Exhibit 5.7. The solver must first change the mixed fractions into improper fractions; second, produce fractions with common denominators; third, add the numerators and place the sum over the common denominator; and fourth, simplify the fraction. Applying this procedure (along with substeps shown in Exhibit 5.7) makes it possible for a student to solve any adding-mixed-fractions problem. Procedures are a second subtype of skill learning.

To summarize, skill questions require the application of a rule or procedure (Gagne, 1985). Don't confuse skill questions with fact questions. One's to know and one's to show. Fact questions require knowledge; skill questions require know-how. Skills must be demonstrated not stated. For example, stating the rules of syllabication is a fact; applying syllabication rules is a skill. Stating the procedure for adding mixed fractions is a fact; applying the adding-mixed-fractions procedure is a skill.

Let's look at some other examples of rules and procedures and then some tips for writing skill questions.

Rules

What is the solution to this problem: 12 + 6 ÷ 3? Is the solution 6 or 14? Do you first add 12 and 6 and then divide the sum by 3 to get 6, or do you first divide 6 by 3 and then add the quotient to 12 to get 14? The correct answer is 14 because there is a rule that governs how to solve this and all other order-of-operations problems. The rule is to conduct mathematical operations in this order: parentheses, exponents, multiplication or division, and addition or subtraction. Therefore, applying the order-of-operations rule leads us to divide before adding.

And how do you make the plural form of words? Here are a few common rules to govern your plural-forming behavior.

- Add *s* to form the plural of most words (e.g., *bug-bugs, cap-caps*).
- Add *es* to words that end in a hissing (*s, z, x, ch, sh*) sound (e.g., *couch-couches, bench-benches*).
- If the word ends in a consonant plus *y*, change the *y* to *ie* and add *s* (e.g., *army-armies, cemetery-cemeteries*).
- If the word ends in *f* or *fe*, change the ending to *ves* (*loaf-loaves, wife-wives*).

From these examples, it is evident that rules are powerful tools for regulating behavior across a wide range of situations. For example, the order of operations rule is applied in any mathematical problem involving multiple operations. A single rule once learned has unlimited utility. It is also evident that rules are composed of concepts. In order to apply the plural rules, you need to recognize singular words and their endings, such as those that end in hissing sounds, a consonant plus *y*, or *f* or *fe*.

Note also, that most rules can be expressed as if/then statements. If a certain condition exists (such as a singular word ending in *f* or *fe*), then you should take a certain course of action (such as changing the ending to *ves*). As other examples, if you see a patrol car up ahead, then you should slow down; if you have a mathematical problem containing parentheses, then you should do what's inside the parentheses first. Recognizing the "if" portion of the rule (e.g., a word ending in *f*, a patrol car, a parentheses) is recognizing a concept. Thus you can see that concept recognition is the first step in applying rules.

Procedures

More complex skills, called procedures, involve the application of two or more steps. For example, the procedure for calculating the hypotenuse of a right triangle is as follows: Square the length of the triangle's base and height, sum the squares, and determine the square root of the summed squares. Carrying out this procedure is not quite as simple as one, two, three, however. The solver must recognize right triangles, base, height, and hypotenuse; square numbers; add numbers; and calculate square roots.

The procedure for calculating the mean of several scores is to add all scores and then divide the sum by the number of scores. This rather simple procedure can become part of a more complex procedure such as calculating standard deviation. Exhibit 5.8 illustrates the procedure for calculating standard deviation. Note that the first step is calculating the mean.

EXHIBIT 5.8   Procedure for Calculating Standard Deviation

	Calculate Mean	Calculate Deviation Scores	Square Deviation Scores	Sum Deviation Scores	Divide Sum by Number of Scores	Find Square Root of Quotient
Example:	Sum of scores divided by number of scores	Mean minus each score				
	13	$9 - 13 = -4$	$-4^2 = 16$	16	$26 \div 5 = 5.2$	$\sqrt{5.2} = 2.28$
	10	$9 - 10 = -1$	$-1^2 = 1$	1		
	8	$9 - 8 = 1$	$1^2 = 1$	1		
	7	$9 - 7 = 2$	$2^2 = 4$	4		
	+7	$9 - 7 = 2$	$2^2 = 4$	+4		
	$45 \div 5 = 9$			26		

Procedures are learned and tested in most academic areas. In math, procedures are used for adding mixed fractions, doing long division, and solving quadratic equations. Scientific procedures include balancing chemical equations, applying the scientific method, and calculating force. In English, grammar and punctuation rules are combined to produce effective writing. And students and teachers can apply SOAR strategies to improve learning and instruction.

Writing Skill Items

When writing skill items to regulate or assess student learning, follow these two item-writing tips. First, be sure items are truly skill items. The question: "What is the formula for calculating the mean?" is a fact question, not a skill question. Students can simply recall provided information from memory. Similarly, having students recognize standard deviation in a table displaying various statistics assesses concept learning; having students calculate standard deviation for a set of numbers assesses skill learning.

Second, provide new problems. If I asked you, "What are the plurals of army and couch?" I am not really assessing skill knowledge because these examples were used during instruction. I must provide new problems such as these: "What is the plural of dairy and church?" Similarly, to assess the skill of calculating standard deviation, a new problem must be presented. When familiar problems are used during testing, the student might recall the solution from memory. In that case, the student is displaying fact rather than skill knowledge.

Postscript

Finally, as students use practice tests to regulate learning, they must realize that practice test items and final test items differ, especially for concept and skill items where new examples and new problems are always used. Memorizing the answers to practice tests has little value. A group of students in my high school biology class learned this lesson the hard way. One student in the class "found" last year's test in a folder, in a drawer, in the teacher's locked desk. The student made the test available to several other students. Some of them used the purloined exam as a practice test. They assessed their current learning and pinpointed areas in need of further study. Others, including the ringleader, assumed the teacher would administer the same test this year, so they tried to memorize the answers to the 30 multiple-choice questions this way: "c, a, b, b, a, d, b, a . . ." Just before the exam, the memorizers were still at it, trying to cram a meandering stream of meaningless letters into their brains. At test time, the instructor announced that he would first hand out the response sheet, make a few test procedure announcements, and then distribute the test. As soon as the response sheet was passed out, one of the brain-stuffed, I've-got-to-get-these-answers-out-now students let out a cry of anguish, thrust an inquiring hand high in the air, and implored, "Can we start?" "Uh, wouldn't you like to wait for the test?" the instructor asked quizzically.

The test, it turned out, was different from last year's. Those who used last year's test to practice and regulate learning did well. Those who memorized answers did poorly. And the student who asked "Can we start?" had a lot of explaining to do during detention.

AIDING REGULATING AFTER INSTRUCTION

At one time I allowed students in my educational psychology course to retake an alternate test if they wanted to try to improve their original test score. The two tests were comparable in form and assessed identical objectives. Following the original test, students' grades were posted by a code number, but the tests were not reviewed in class or returned.

Students wanting to review their test could do so privately in my office. Now, here is the shocker. About half of the students who chose to retake the test never came to my office to go over their original test. They took the retake exam knowing their original score but not which items they missed. Guess how they performed. That's right; performance was about the same on the retake test as on the original. In fact, students missed comparable items from one test to the other. Students had a golden opportunity to learn from their mistakes but let the opportunity slide. That's because students often hide from their mistakes. They find it painful to review missed test items or teacher comments even though those missed items and comments hold the key to improvement. Successful learners stare down their mistakes and perceive defeat as opportunity. Recall that the Wright brothers' made many mistakes but used those mistakes as opportunities to learn. It was correcting mistakes that got the Wright brothers airborne.

For students to learn from their mistakes, teachers must do more than provide student scores. Errors must be analyzed to determine what went wrong and why. More specifically, students need to know the error content, type, and source. The content pertains to the topic of the test question. Perhaps the question covered Pythagoras's theorem. The type of question pertains to whether the question measured fact, concept, or skill learning. The test item "What is the formula for finding the hypotenuse of a right triangle?" is, for example, a fact item. The error source refers to why the error occurred. The primary source might be a gap or error in the student's knowledge base. For example, perhaps the student confused Pythagoras's theorem with Pascal's triangle. The secondary source pinpoints why the error occurred. According to the SOAR model, an error might occur because of a failure to select and note key ideas, organize ideas, create associations, or regulate learning. Perhaps, in this case, the student failed to select and note the definition. Let's look at a student's marked test and what can be learned through error analysis.

Test on Perimeter and Area

1. What is the formula for calculating the perimeter of a rectangle?

2. What is the formula for calculating the area of a rectangle?

3. Which of these shaded figures represents the area of the rectangle?

4. Which figure below highlights the perimeter of the rectangle?

Calculate the perimeter for each rectangle below.

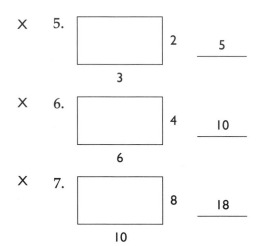

Calculate the area for each rectangle below.

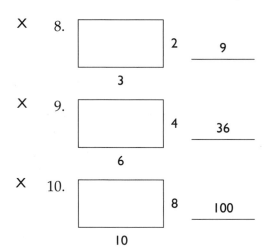

The student missed 6 of the 10 test questions and scored 40%, but that single score hardly tells the story of what the student knows, doesn't know, and needs to learn. Exhibit 5.9 shows an error analysis matrix for this student that pinpoints problems and solutions. From this analysis,

| EXHIBIT 5.9 | Error Analysis Matrix for Perimeter and Area Test |

Item Number	Type	Content
1	Fact	Perimeter
2	Fact	Area
3	Concept	Area
4	Concept	Perimeter
✗ 5	Skill	Perimeter
✗ 6	Skill	Perimeter
✗ 7	Skill	Perimeter
✗ 8	Skill	Area
✗ 9	Skill	Area
✗ 10	Skill	Area

it's easy to see what went wrong. In terms of error type, the student performed flawlessly on fact and concept items but missed all six skill items. The student could state the perimeter and area definitions (fact), recognize examples (concept), but could not calculate perimeter or area (skill). In terms of error content, skill errors occurred for both perimeter and area content. To determine error source, look closely at the student's errors and see if a pattern emerges. Did you notice that the errors are systematic? For all the perimeter calculation problems, the student is adding length plus width but is failing to double the sum. For all the area calculation problems, the student is multiplying opposite sides (length × length) rather than multiplying the adjacent sides (length × width). It is fairly common for students to state a formula correctly (fact knowledge) but apply it incorrectly (skill knowledge). To uncover the secondary source of the student's errors will take some detective work. We would likely find complete and accurate notes (selection) but a failure to practice the skills accurately or sufficiently (regulation). The student also probably needed to better associate the perimeter and area skills to their formula and to one another.

Learning does not end when the last answer is penciled in. Tests are yield signs, not stop signs. Teachers should help students regulate understanding even after learning is assessed. Much can be learned by analyzing test errors. Teachers and students can determine the content, type, and source of student errors. As a result, knowledge gaps and error patterns are uncovered. Students can then fill those gaps, correct faulty patterns, and master the content. It's never too late to learn. For such learning to occur, however, teachers must do more than report test scores. They must help students engage in error analysis. And students cannot shy away from feedback. Instead, they must seize it and exploit it.

STRATEGY INSTRUCTION: TEACHING STUDENTS TO REGULATE

Here is an example of how a language arts teacher might teach students the strategy of creating practice tests to regulate learning.

"Class, next week you will be tested over two objectives. Let's revisit those objectives."

- Given a variety of figure-of-speech examples (alliteration, onomatopoeia, oxymoron, hyperbole, metaphor, and simile), the student will recognize each type, with 80% accuracy.
- Given a number of unmarked sentences, the student will supply the correct ending punctuation mark (period, question mark, or exclamation point), with 80% accuracy.

"Many of you are going to walk into that test and let me be the first one to test you. That's academic suicide and should never happen. You should test yourself so thoroughly in advance that there is nothing I can ask you that you haven't already asked yourself. If you do that, you'll know whether or not you know everything you need to know. And if you don't know everything, you have time to do something about it." (*Sell the strategy*)

"This is exactly what champion sports teams do. They figure out what their opponents have in store for them before the game even starts, and they practice accordingly. If they know the opposition plays a box-in-one defense, they practice against this defense and prepare to exploit it." (*Sell the strategy*)

"The best strategy for you to use to make sure you're ready for the test is to develop a practice test. Let me show you how. Take a look at the practice test I developed for you. It pertains to the first objective on figures of speech. The objective called for you to recognize new figure-of-speech examples so the practice test asks you to do just that. To make sure you can meet the objective, the practice test provides a lot of new examples to recognize. In creating it, I was careful not to use any class examples you've already seen." (*Introduce the strategy*)

"Now, let's have you practice. Work with a partner to construct a practice test that covers the second test objective on punctuation.

Pay close attention to the objective, and be sure your test matches the objective. Your practice test must provide a variety of unmarked sentences and require the insertion of ending punctuation marks." (*Perfect the strategy*)

"The practice test strategy can be used anywhere. You can use it when preparing for any academic test, preparing for a speech or a music recital, or when readying for an athletic contest." (*Generalize the strategy*)

Interlude

Congratulations on completing the first five chapters of *Teaching How to Learn.* To this point you've learned how to help students select, organize, associate, and regulate (SOAR) like Teacher A does and how to teach students to SOAR like Teacher A+ does. That's quite an accomplishment, but that's still not enough. Three support chapters follow, covering motivation, behavior management, and extraordinary capabilities. Here's why. Students who are not motivated to soar remain grounded. That's why Chapter 6 covers motivation. You'll learn how to motivate students and how to teach them to motivate themselves. Students who are off task—not doing what they should be doing—cannot soar either. That's why Chapter 7 covers behavior management. You'll learn how to manage student behavior and how to teach students to manage themselves. And because there is no limit to how high students can soar, Chapter 8 covers how to make students extraordinary—or at least more extraordinary. When all is said and done, you'll fully be able to help students soar to success and beyond.

Before moving ahead, check out the following recap. It selects, organizes, and associates the key information from the first five chapters and provides questions to help you regulate your learning.

A SOAR RECAP OF CHAPTERS 1–5

Select and Organize

	Select	Organize	Associate	Regulate
		SOAR Strategies		
What students do wrong:	Misfocus attention and record incomplete notes	Construct lists and outlines	Piecemeal learning	Redundant strategies
How Teacher A can help:	Provide notes, frameworks, and cues. Repeat lesson and encourage reconstruction.	Provide hierarchy, sequence, matrix, and illustration representations.	Raise association questions, anchor instruction, provide examples, provide mnemonics, and use representations to build associations.	Provide objectives, rubrics, timelines,and practice tests. Conduct error analysis.
How Teacher A+ can teach students how to learn:	———————— Embed SOAR Strategy Instruction ————————			

Associate

- Students make learning errors across the SOAR board; each error type is repaired by a SOAR strategy.
- Teacher A develops effective instruction that helps students SOAR; Teacher A+ teaches students how to SOAR.
- Representations are the cornerstone of learning. They aid selection. Cues and frameworks signal matrix topics and categories; complete notes can appear in matrix form. They aid organization. Representations organize information in hierarchies, sequences, matrices, and illustrations. They aid association. Representations are analyzed to reveal associations.

They aid regulation. Potential test questions arise from representations, and error analysis profiles are written in matrix form.

• Strategy instruction is akin to counseling. In both cases, the goal is to solve an immediate problem and to offset a potential long-range one.

Regulate

1. What are four learning errors students commit?

2. Use the puzzle analogy to explain why piecemeal learning is ineffective.

3. What does strategy instruction have to do with fishing?

4. List five things teachers can do to improve selection?

5. Name the four types of representations and the type of relationship each conveys.

6. Name the five ways recommended for fostering associations.

7. Identify the following examples as fact, concept, or skill learning:
   a. Recognizing the song of the whip-poor-will on a walk through the woods
   b. Listing the names and term dates of the first 10 presidents
   c. Correcting grammar errors in a new sentence

8. Based on Kohlberg's theory of moral development shown below, help students associate and regulate learning.

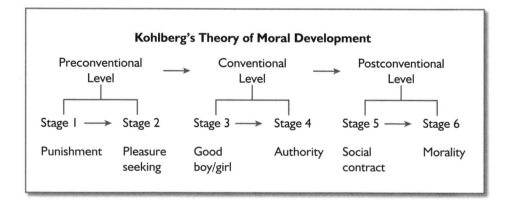

PART II

Support Strategies

6

Helping Students Motivate

Have you ever pondered running the Boston Marathon, swimming the English Channel, climbing Mount Everest, or doing your own taxes? Pretty frightening stuff. For most of us, these unimaginable ventures seem far beyond our reach. But even the unimaginable becomes possible when motivation propels us. Let me tell you the story of Dick Hoyt and what motivation propelled him to accomplish (Reilly, 2005). Dick Hoyt was a sedentary man who had never run more than a mile, had never learned to swim, and had not ridden a bicycle since he was six years old. Dick's teenage son, Rick, was wheelchair bound and could not speak. Rick's high school classmate was paralyzed in an accident, and a five-mile charity run was organized on his behalf. Rick typed the message, "Dad, I want to do that." Dick mustered the motivation and strength to push himself and his son through the race. Rick found the run exhilarating; Dick found it painful for two weeks. Afterward, Rick typed, "Dad, when we were running, it felt like I wasn't disabled anymore." And that sentence became Dick's motivation to push, pull, and carry his son to places few can imagine. Since that five-mile race, the pair has completed 85 marathons, 212 triathlons, scaled mountains, cross-country skied, and biked across America. There is no stopping motivation.

Success stems from two factors: skill and will (motivation). An effective student possesses academic skills, such as the SOAR skills described in this text. Those skills mean little, however, if the student lacks the will to employ the SOAR skills. Both skill and will are needed. This chapter is about the will or motivation essential for success. In this chapter, you'll learn about motivation's four factors: desire, intention, focus, and sustain. The first letters of these factors spell DIFS. You can remember this because "DIFS makes the difference." DIFS is the difference between failure and success. Another way to remember DIFS is the sentence, "Do it for success." Motivation's four factors—desire, intention, focus, and sustain—help you do it for success.

A teacher can boost motivation at any stage, during or throughout the DIFS process. To help you, Exhibit 6.1 presents the DIFS Will Riser. It is a planning and record-keeping device, which can be completed by student and teacher. To demonstrate how the DIFS Will Riser works to help an unmotivated student learn about health, it is applied at the end of each DIFS section.

EXHIBIT 6.1   The DIFS Will Riser

DESIRE

Internal Boosters
   Emotional arousal:
   Consciousness-raising:
   Models:

External Boosters—Rewards:
Goal Statements
   Short-range:
   Long-range:

INTENTION

Plan for Success:
Plan a Foundation
   Environmental supports:
   Social supports:
Plan Time:

FOCUS

Launch Date:
Record Progress:
Counter Obstacles:

SUSTAIN

Reward Behavior:
Make Lifestyle Changes:

DESIRE

Motivation begins with desire. Dick Hoyt never scales a mountain, pedals across America, battles an ocean current, or races the Boston Marathon without the desire to please his son and help him feel whole. Ralph Waldo Emerson said, "What lies behind us and what lies before us are small matters compared to what lies within us."

Desire comes from two places: inside and outside. Inside desire—also called *intrinsic motivation*—stems from enjoying the activity. Outside desire—also called *extrinsic motivation*—stems from external rewards. Although inside desire is best, both are powerful motivators (Pintrich & Schunk, 1996).

Inside Desire

If you are going to pursue something, it's best if you enjoy the path. That way, even if you never quite reach your goal, the trip was worthwhile. Author Louis L'Amour said, "The trail is the thing, not the end of the trail." Success is in the journey, not the destination.

I remember that it was inside desire that moved me to resign my third-grade teaching position and attend graduate school full time. I hungered to study educational psychology. I knew that if I fell short of earning my PhD, I would still relish the time spent learning.

Now, as an educational psychologist, I'm interested in talent and expertise, so I conducted research on teenage chess masters, all of whom were boys, to find out how they got to be so good so fast (Kiewra, O'Connor, McCrudden, & Liu, 2006). I found that most of them study or play chess 10 to 20 hours a week. I asked their parents why the young masters work so hard at chess: Was it the prestige or the trophies? No, not at all. Every parent offered the same basic answer: "He just loves it. He just loves playing and studying chess. It's his passion."

When people are fueled by inside desire, there is no stopping them. Dick Hoyt was told that he could not push a wheelchair in the Boston Marathon, but he did it anyway—unofficially. Later, he found a way to enter his son and himself officially—by the pair meeting Boston's stringent qualifying time of 2:50, a standard that keeps many serious, non-wheelchair-pushing runners from competing.

Not all people have this sort of desire. Fortunately, there are four things teachers can do that might ignite inside desire: consciousness-raising, emotional arousal, modeling, and mastery orientation. Each technique is described and then exemplified for the health topic of automobile safety.

Consciousness-Raising

The term *consciousness-raising* was popularized in the 1960s when radical feminists set out to inform society that women were oppressed. Their data, stories, and fiery bras raised American's consciousness and internally motivated many people to fight for women's rights. Certainly, there are other examples of national consciousness-raising, including the civil rights movement and the surgeon general's warnings about the dangers of cigarette smoking. Knowledge is power. Information is often the engine that drives people to action (see Prochaska, Norcross, & DiClemente, 2002).

A health teacher who wants to motivate teens to drive safely might provide sobering information like the following:

- Motor vehicle crashes are the leading cause of death among teenagers.
- Teens are involved in three times as many fatal crashes as other drivers.
- Sixty five percent of all teen passenger deaths occur when another teen is driving.
- Teenage driving deaths increase with each additional passenger.
- Failure to wear seat belts contributes to more fatalities than any other factor.
- Teens have the lowest seatbelt use among all drivers.

Emotional Arousal

Did the story about Dick Hoyt inspire you to get up from the couch and exercise? Did it motivate you to do more for your child than play Monopoly or order pizza? Emotional experiences—in the form of verbal or visual stories—can jump-start desire (Prochaska et al., 2002). I began running in 1978 because of two emotional experiences. The first was an article I read about the Long Island Marathon and several runners who competed. I was moved by the runners' training commitment and their ability to run further than I care to drive. The second was the film *Rocky*. The scenes where Rocky slurped raw eggs, punched raw meat, ran the streets of historic Philadelphia, and transformed himself from a bum to a champion were the fuel that ignited 30 years of running (and an odd disdain for raw eggs and beef).

A health teacher can arouse emotions that motivate teens to drive safely. The instructor can show horrifying crash images and relate devastating testimonials from maimed survivors or those who endure the loss of a loved one. The archives of any local newspaper contain sad and shocking stories of teen deaths caused by reckless driving or failure to wear seat belts.

Modeling

People imitate models—particularly those of high status (Pintrich & Schunk, 1996, chap. 5). Kids once wore coonskin caps, just like Davy

Crockett. When the Beatles invaded the United States, mop top hairstyles were the rage. Remember the Marlboro Man? He was probably responsible for more American deaths than the Vietnam War. Today, Tiger Woods is making Nike cash registers ring by modeling their latest gear and driving a Nike brand golf ball. And millions of Americans swallow the latest diet craze and hit the gym for a spin on the treadmill and some abdominal tightening trying to imitate the fit looking models splashed on television screens and magazine covers.

Teen driving is influenced by modeling—both negatively and positively. When teen heroes—such as recording artists, actors, and athletes—drive recklessly, teens are, unfortunately, apt to imitate them. Teens are also likely to model peers who drive dangerously and parents who do not wear seat belts. But safe driving can be increased through modeling too. Teens naturally should be taught to drive by adults who model safe practices. And health instructors can recruit local heroes from schools and the community to recount their own safe driving attitudes and behaviors.

Mastery Orientation

Mastery-oriented teachers ignite inside desire by helping students focus on material mastery and personal growth rather than competition for grades, smiley faces, or other tangible rewards. Teachers can foster mastery in the following ways:

- Emphasize the real world benefits of learning.
- Make learning enjoyable.
- Help students work cooperatively rather than competitively.
- Measure students' performance in relationship to preset standards rather than to other students' performance.
- Permit retesting without penalty.
- Permit more time to learn if needed.

Under mastery conditions, students need not worry about tests, grades, competition, and time constraints. Instead, they focus on learning benefits and are internally motivated to make progress toward mastery.

The mastery-oriented health teacher emphasizes that the course material on automobile safety is not about grades but about attaining an important and enjoyable life skill that is also fraught with danger. The instructor lays out clear objectives at the outset and helps students meet them. There are assessments, but these mark progress and are repeated until mastery is met. The course might incorporate relevant and enjoyable practice on a driving simulator. And when students practice they cooperate by offering corrective feedback and advice.

Outside Desire

Sometimes people lack internal desire. How about you? Do you enjoy work, working out, or cutting the grass? When you don't enjoy doing something, how do you muster the motivation to do it? When passion fizzles, external rewards make motivation sizzle (Skinner, 1953). You might hate your job, but paychecks and health plan benefits keep you punching the clock. You might despise elliptical machines, stair climbers, barbells, and sweat, but improved health indices and complements keep you working out. You might want to cut lawn maintenance from your summer schedule, but outside benefits such as weed and bug control and a showcase lawn keep you mowing.

Instructors should use external rewards to flame desire when internal desire won't burn. As a reward for effective performance, students can be given tangible items such as high grades, stickers, gold stars, free time, no-homework coupons, merit certificates, extra recess, parties, and positive notes home. These external rewards should increase desire for the time being. External rewards might even boost internal desire as students come to enjoy the activity. A possible downside is that external rewards often lack the staying power of internal ones. When the external reward is withheld or has lost its luster, behavior falls.

Goal Statements

Whether students' desire stems from inside or outside, it's important they channel and express that desire with goal statements that specify what's to be accomplished (see Pintrich & Schunk, 1996, chap. 6, for a discussion of goals). Political strategist Scott Reed said, "One step—choosing a goal and sticking to it—changes everything." Without goals, people tend to drift like balloons riding changing currents. Goal statements direct effort. They are the bull's-eye to aim at, the North Star to follow. Teachers should help students develop goal statements that are challenging, short range and long range, and public.

Challenging Goals

Architect Daniel Burnham said, "Make no little plans; they have no magic. . . . Make big plans, aim high in hope and work." You've heard of the American dream? You get a job, get married, buy a house in the suburbs, and bear 2.3 children. That dream could be a nightmare. What if your job is washroom attendant at a Laundromat? What if your spouse turns up on an episode of *America's Most Wanted*? What if your house was built on a methane dump? And what if your kids get stuck playing right field or land only supporting roles in the school play? To jump high, you must aim high. As motivational speaker Les Brown said, "No one rises to low expectations. . . . If you go through life being casual; you'll end up a casualty."

So develop challenging goals. The goal is not to land any job but to find or create one that is both personally and financially rewarding, not to get married but to wed someone you love and cherish, not to buy a house but a home that is stout and comforting, and not to bear 2.3 children when 2.8 is well within range.

You get the idea, help students set challenging goals. Why "stay in school" when excelling at school is doable? Cockroaches can stay in school. Why "say no to drugs" when saying "yes to a healthy lifestyle" is better yet? Why read a chapter when fully comprehending it is moments away? Einstein set lofty scientific goals (his hair-grooming goals were obviously more lax) and criticized colleagues for their meager goals. He said, "I have no respect for scientists who take a board of wood, look for its thinnest part, and drill a great many holes where drilling is easy."

Short- and Long-Range Goals

A lot of students don't know what they want to be when they grow up. Heck, a lot of grown-ups share this uncertainty. It's okay to be uncertain about the future, but it's not okay to be goalless. The goalless wander and have trouble finding the path. Sari was a high school student who had no aspirations for college or a career. She wanted to get through high school, get her own place, and get any job that paid the rent. Well, she got through high school with a 2.0 average and began working for minimum wage cleaning up after sick animals at a veterinarian hospital. Then something happened. She found she loved working with animals and soon set her first real goal: earning a bachelor's degree in the rigorous field of veterinarian science. Sari applied for admission to the state college's veterinarian program but was denied because of low grades. Sari had wandered too far from the path and was lost. While in high school, Sari should have minimally set and pursued some generic, short-range goals such as earning high grades, participating in clubs and activities, and volunteering time in the community. Accomplishing these goals would have made her a better candidate for college or employment. When setting long-range goals is not feasible, setting and pursuing challenging, short-range goals keeps one on or near potential pathways. The metaphorical advice in baseball is "cover your bases."

Although setting and meeting short-range goals keeps you in the game, it is best to set long-range goals too—even if they might change. Here's why. Long-range goals dictate short-range goals. If the long-range goal is to be a professional writer, then obvious short-range goals include studying literature and composition, and practicing writing most every day. If the long-range goal is a political career, then obvious short-range goals include studying political science, gaining political experience, and keeping skeletons from your closet. Long-range goals dictate short-range goals, which specify how to live your life today. And how you spend your days is how you spend your life.

Involve students in an important goal setting activity by having them periodically complete the goals matrix in Exhibit 6.2. Students first contemplate and record potential long-range career, academic, and personal goals. Next, they contemplate and record potential short-range goals in those same areas. When examining the completed matrix, look for goal integration. Short-range goals should feed into long-range goals; academic, career, and personal goals should be compatible. The academic goal of completing college, the career goal of becoming a teacher, and the personal goal of spending a lot of time with family are highly compatible. Earning a high school diploma, becoming CEO of a *Fortune* 500 company, and spending a lot of time with family are not compatible goals. When goals are at odds, pursuing one might actually pull you from another.

EXHIBIT 6.2   Goal-Setting Matrix

	GOALS		
	Academic	*Career*	*Personal*
Short range:			
Long range:			

Public Goals

Encourage students to make goals public. They need not post them on the Internet for the cyberworld to see, but sharing them with family, teachers, teammates, or friends serves two purposes. First, the public goal setter is likely to work harder to meet the goal knowing that others are watching. Second, the public can offer support in the form of guidance or encouragement. My college English professor told me that he once had serious doubts about his goal to begin a doctoral program because he was already 36 years old. He shared his goal and doubts with his father saying, "It'll take four years to get the degree. I'd be 40 when I graduate." His father offered this sage advice, "Son, the way I figure it, you'll be 40 in four years anyway—with or without your doctorate."

Counsel students who are reluctant to publicize their goals to post them privately. Posted goals remind you where you are headed. When I began running, my goal was to run a sub-three-hour marathon. I wrote this goal on index cards and posted them on my nightstand to boost motivation when the alarm sounded at 5:00 a.m. for a training run and on my refrigerator to discourage unnecessary snacking. Students can easily post course goals on the inside covers of notebooks and plan books to rekindle their desire. Paul H. Nitze, former Secretary of the Navy, said, "One of the most dangerous forms of human error is forgetting what one is trying to achieve."

Using the DIFS Will Riser to Boost Desire

Troy is not motivated to learn about health. He finds the topic boring and unrelated to his life, even though he enjoys sports and hopes to some-day play high school basketball. Troy's health teacher, Ms. Perkins, uses the DIFS Will Riser shown in Exhibit 6.1 to boost Troy's desire. Ms. Perkins begins by supplying internal boosters. She arouses Troy's emotions by showing video clips of basketball players making spectacular shots and dunks. She raises Troy's health consciousness by revealing sobering statistics about teen obesity, drug addiction, and driving accidents. And she calls upon a basketball-playing role model from the local college to reveal his healthy habits. As an external reward for performing well in health class, Ms. Perkins arranges for Troy to attend a basketball practice at the local college and meet the players. Finally, she and Troy develop short- and long-range health goals. Troy's short-range goals are to earn at least a B in health class and to follow a healthier lifestyle now in terms of diet and exercise. Troy's long-range goal is to lead the kind of healthy life conducive to playing high school basketball. Goal cards are made and displayed in Troy's room and in his locker.

INTENTION

Don't be afraid of the space between your dreams and reality. If you can dream it, you can make it so.

—Belva Davis, broadcast journalist

Intention is planning to meet the goal, to live the dream. Too often, goals are aborted and dreams are spoiled because there is no plan for reaching them. Just as builders need plans to construct a dream house, students need plans to fulfill their dreams. Help students draft plans that fulfill these conditions: Plan for success, plan a foundation, and plan time.

Plan for Success

An acquaintance had met the girl of his dreams and proposed marriage. Before the ceremony, he directed his attorney to draft a prenuptial agreement that specified the division of property should the marriage fail. And fail it did. One might argue that the acquaintance planned for marital failure, not marital bliss. Rather than plan for marriage dissolution, he should have planned for marriage resolution: a joint bank account, adjacent cemetery plots, and even a common cell phone plan (there is no getting out of that).

Pessimists rarely succeed. Helen Keller said, "No pessimist ever discovered the secrets of the stars or sailed to an uncharted land or opened a new heaven to the human spirit." Optimists believe they can succeed and do. Ernest Holmes, a spiritual philosopher, said, "Believe as though you are, and you will be." An Arabic proverb advises: "Throw your heart in front of you and run ahead and catch it."

Get students to think optimistically about meeting goals and fulfilling dreams. One way is to show them models of others who succeeded. In the 1950s, no runner had ever broken four minutes for the mile. Runners thought it could not be done. Finally, Englishman Roger Bannister cracked the four-minute barrier. Soon afterward, several runners—even grandmothers and pastry chefs—broke four minutes. Seeing was believing. Once they saw others reach the goal, they believed they could too.

In the movie *Stand and Deliver,* math teacher Jaime Escalante uses modeling to convince his dropout prone students that they can master calculus, earn college scholarships to top schools, and land high paying corporate jobs. He invites those who already earned success in his class to return and visit current students. The visitors park their fancy cars in view, wear designer suits, and spin their success stories. They are living testaments that success is attainable.

Plan a Foundation

I have a friend who is really good at quitting smoking; he's quit six times! When seeking long-term success—regular exercise, a healthy diet, safe driving practices, daily reading, saving for retirement, optimal job performance, or quitting smoking—success is often temporary. Adherence is difficult. That's because most success plans rest on a shaky foundation. Just as a house must be built on a strong foundation, so must plans for success.

One woman hoped to become more active and fit. She planned to start walking and running and even compete in some local fun runs. She thought this would be a good way to feel and look better. Good plan—so far. The woman, meanwhile, wanted to maintain other lifestyle habits. She wasn't willing to change her unhealthy eating habits, curtail drinking, or quit smoking. She sought advice on how much physical activity was necessary to overcome the rest of her lifestyle. A plan for regular exercise built on a decadent lifestyle was not going to take this woman far. Her exercise plan needed to rest on a sturdy foundation that could support it. Like it or not, she needed to build a foundation or support structure for regular exercise.

Support structures (Prochaska et al., 2002) are environmental and social. The exercise planner should seek environmental supports like health clubs, health food stores, exercise and nutrition books, and fun run activities. Environments that cater to smoking and drinking should be avoided. The exercise planner should seek social supports such as running clubs and exercise partners. "Old friends" that can lead one off course should be avoided. As Les Brown said, "If you run with losers, you'll become a loser" and "You can run faster with 100 people that want to go, than with one hanging around your neck."

Help students plan a stout foundation for academic success. Environmental supports might include study space, technology equipment and programs, study materials, and time. Distracting environments should be avoided. Social supports might include a study buddy, study group, and a teacher or parent helper. Fellow students wanting to socialize or complain about the course should be avoided, as should those who are ill prepared and can only share ignorance instead of knowledge.

Plan Time

Remember what The Rolling Stones said about time? "Time is on our side, oh yes it is." When it comes to planning for success, time is a great ally. That's because success depends on spending a lot of time, beginning today, most every day. Let's examine these three time factors.

Author Beryl Markham said, "If a man has any greatness in him, it comes to light—not in one flamboyant hour, but in the ledger of his daily work." How do talented individuals get to be so good so fast? The answer is they really don't. Talent is not inborn. Talent takes time—even for the most prodigious like Mozart in music, Picasso in art, and Bobby Fischer in chess. As you'll learn in Chapter 8, a lot of practice, over many years, yields talent.

Plan to get started now. Former Supreme Court Justice Sandra Day O'Connor said, "Slaying the dragon of delay is no sport for the short-winded." The cost of a college education is astronomical and rising faster than a diver with a broken air hose. For a child born today, I believe the projected cost of a college education is $35 million dollars . . . plus books and fees. The only way to finance a college education, without counterfeiting, is to begin saving today.

Once in college, many students procrastinate when it comes to completing school work or meeting other goals. One interviewer asked college students if they procrastinate. Twelve percent immediately said no, 46% thought they did, and 42% said they'd tell the interviewer later. Procrastination, though, is like a credit card. It's a lot of fun until you get the bill.

Teachers should advise students to begin assignments, test preparation, and other goal-directed actions right away. A goal completion timeline, like that in Exhibit 6.3, helps students get started early and invest time regularly. Students should also understand that later is better than never. Although the best time to plant a tree was 20 years ago, the next best time is today.

EXHIBIT 6.3   Goal Completion Timeline for a Term Paper

Date:	Sept. 15	Sept. 30	Oct. 10	Oct. 25	Nov. 8	Nov. 24
Task:	Choose topic	Review literature	Organize paper	Write first draft	Write second draft	Write final draft

Plan to invest time regularly. Regular time investments—even small ones—pay off. Some people read 15 to 20 books a year—and I'm not just talking about people with a lot of time on their hands like subsidized farmers and Alaskan lifeguards; I'm talking about busy people like you. Most do it by reading 15 to 30 minutes each night before nodding off to sleep. Advise students aiming at distant goals—a midterm exam in six weeks, a project due next month, or a horn solo in the May concert—to plan regular and steady time investments.

Help students recognize that goal completion plans might also incorporate spare moments often frittered away throughout the day—time wasted waiting for a bus, riding to school, waiting for class to start, or enduring television commercials. These small time pockets hold opportunity to chip away at goals. In just a few minutes, students can chip away at reading or homework assignments or study using SOAR strategies.

Using the DIFS Will Riser to Boost Intention

Ms. Perkins uses the DIFS Will Riser in Exhibit 6.1 to help Troy make plans for course success and a healthier lifestyle. Ms. Perkins helps Troy plan for success by showing him course and health performance data from past years. She shares a summary of course grades showing that most students earned an A or B. She also shares project data showing that 95% of students improved health habits related to diet, exercise, or safety. Overall, these data convince Troy that health success is possible. Ms. Perkins also helps Troy plan a foundation for success. She offers environmental supports, such as times the school and community gymnasiums are open for recreation, a list of healthy food options on the school menu, and a copy of the basketball schedules for the local high school and college teams. Ms. Perkins encourages Troy to use social supports such as his parents, who can help plan and prepare healthy meals, and his classmates, who can be exercise buddies and healthy-food-choice lunch mates. Finally, Ms. Perkins helps Troy plan time. Together they construct a timeline plan matrix, like that in Exhibit 6.4, with days listed across the top, exercise, diet, and study time listed as categories down the left margin, and matrix cells containing daily goals.

EXHIBIT 6.4	Timeline Planning Matrix for Meeting Health Goals

	Sunday	Monday	Tuesday	Wednesday	Thursday	Friday	Saturday
Exercise:							
Diet:							
Study time:							

FOCUS

Knowledge of the path cannot be substituted for putting one foot in front of the other.

—M. C. Richards, artist and teacher

It's time to turn plans into action. It's time to put one foot in front of the other. Focus is concentrated action toward a goal while countering obstacles in the path.

Concentrated action begins by getting started, but getting started today is never easy while tomorrow beckons. Untold dreams have withered and died on tomorrow's doorstep while opportunity knocks today. The "I'll get started tomorrow" mantra likely stems from fear and anxiety. Goal setters fear they'll fall short of their goal or are anxious about sacrificing their familiar, secure lifestyle—even though change is for the better. Fear and anxiety paralyze many in the starting blocks who wait for "just the right time to begin." People wait for summer . . . or for autumn, winter, or spring. They wait for "things to slow down" or for pressure to build up. But goal setters should set a launch date and stick to it come heat or high water. Author Johann Wolfgang Von Goethe said, "Whatever you can do, or dream you can, begin it. . . . Seize this very minute. Boldness has genius, power, and magic in it; only engage and then the mind grows heated. Begin, and then the work will be completed." The philosopher Hillel said simply, "If now is not the time to act, when will it be?"

Breaking ground is vital but so are the many spades of dirt that follow. Much work is necessary. Psychologist Anders Ericsson found practice time was the key to success across several domains (Ericsson, 1996). Even among highly accomplished musicians, the more they practiced, the better they performed. Remember that talent does not come in a flash of inspiration but in the ledger of daily work. Author Jeffery Archer captured the importance of hard work and put talent in its place. He said, "Never be frightened of those you assume have more talent than you do, because in the end energy will prevail. My formula is this: Energy plus talent and you are king; energy and no talent and you are still a prince; talent and no energy and you are a pauper." Author Sarah Brown captured the importance of hard work in a fowl way. She said, "The only thing that ever sat its way to success was a hen."

One helpful way to stay focused is to record daily progress. That little tic mark alongside a completed goal on a goal list or that small notation on a calendar showing the day's practice time and methods are marks of triumph, footprints on the road to success. They also are data points for determining if practice methods are working.

The focused worker must counter obstacles. The biggest obstacles are distractions that pull goal seekers from their path. Clergyman and author Henry Emerson Fosdick cautioned, "No steam or gas drives anything unless it is confined. No life ever grows great until it is focused, dedicated, disciplined." Goal seekers must sometimes say "no" and turn their backs on competing opportunities in order to stay on track. Psychologist Mihaly Csikszentmihalyi (1996) studied highly productive people and found that they commonly ignored things that interfered with their work. One individual, who was asked to participate in the study, wrote: "I hope you will not think me presumptuous or rude if I say that one of the secrets of productivity is to have a VERY BIG waste paper basket to take care of ALL invitations such as yours—productivity in my experience consists of NOT doing anything that helps the work of other people but to spend one's time on the work the good Lord has fitted one to do, and do it well" (p. 14). Les Brown concurs, saying, "When not pursuing your goal, you are committing spiritual suicide."

Have students check periodically to be sure they are on track. A colleague of mine did just that. He composed two lists. The first recounted his goals and priorities. The second chronicled how he was actually spending time. He noticed that the two lists were at odds. He was not focused on his goals. For instance, he valued religion but spent little time at church or in prayer. He had begun writing a book but was spending little time working on it. He valued fitness but worked out infrequently. He noticed a lot of time drainers inconsistent with his goals—such as committee meetings, travel time, and television viewing. Seeing all this, he opted off several committees, used travel time to dictate notes for his book, limited television time, and made time for exercise and spiritual renewal. He took hold of his life and better focused his efforts. He put his time where his goals were.

Distractions are not the only obstacles. Barriers come in all shapes and sizes. No matter, goal seekers must find their way over, under, around, or through barriers. They must not be deterred. Publilius Syrus, who wrote in the first century B.C., said, "Anyone can hold the helm when the sea is calm." Next, two more common barriers and how to bypass them are discussed: doubt and bad situations.

If you believe you can, you can; if you doubt you can, you can't. Doubt stems from past experiences and misguided beliefs. I doubt I can fix a car because I never have before. Moreover, my father sent me subtle messages as a kid that I was not mechanically inclined, "You're putting wiper fluid in the radiator, you lunkhead. Get away from the car before you ruin it." Students often have misguided beliefs about ability. They believe, for example, that intelligence is inborn and fixed. They don't realize that intelligence is influenced largely by environment. Animals and people reared in more loving and stimulating environments are generally smarter than those from impoverished environments. The same goes for athletic, musical, mathematical, and mechanical abilities. Students believe these are inborn and fixed, but they too are modifiable. Regardless of genetic potential, anyone can make great strides in athletics or hit the high notes in music given proper training and practice (see Ericsson, 1996). Taken together, past experiences and misguided beliefs often render dangerous self-doubt concoctions such as, "I can't learn trigonometry. I'm not mathematically inclined." "I don't have an athletic bone in my body. I've never done well in sports and never will." "I'm a lousy student and always will be. I'm just stupid."

Overcoming the doubt barrier requires accurate information about ability and small successes that alter history. Students need to know that ability is like a rubber band. At birth, we are issued different sized ability bands. But environmental factors such as instruction and practice can stretch those bands to great lengths. Our potential to grow rests more in our own hands than the seeds of our parents. Small successes can boost self-confidence, too. Should I someday succeed in adding wiper fluid and inflating the tires, then changing the oil suddenly seems possible. Teachers, then, must erase doubt—by assuring students that they are at the helm and by charting a course that students can navigate successfully. A student seeking a musical goal, for example, must be persuaded that success stems from musical training and practice, not musical genes. The teacher must also arrange the environment so that small, but ever increasing, successes are found along the goal path.

There are plenty of bad situations: families encumbered by unemployment, low crop yield, a hurricane, a plummeting investment, racism, or a string of bad luck. Sometimes, people blame their bad situation for their misfortunate lot in life. Talk shows and courtrooms are overrun with people blaming others for their misfortunes. With blame comes the abdication of responsibility, the loss of hope, and yet another "somebody done me wrong" country song.

The Blame Game is not functional. It excuses blamers from what ails them and provides no remedy for success. Here are two examples. David MacEnulty was hired to teach chess at an elementary school in the South

Bronx in New York City—a place with one of the highest poverty and crime rates in the United States. The children who joined the chess club knew little or nothing about the game and were soundly beaten when they played in local tournaments against more seasoned players. MacEnulty's group could have easily tipped their kings and resigned from chess. After all, these were children from bad situations: single-family homes, welfare, or a relative in jail. MacEnulty, though, convinced them that their weak play stemmed not from bad situations but from a lack of instruction and practice. Chess pieces don't care about your color, tax bracket, or where you come from, MacEnulty told them. The children kept pushing pawns and continued to learn and practice. In just a few years, MacEnulty's chess children won city, state, and national titles. Their amazing story was chronicled in a television movie called *Knights of the South Bronx*.

Shelby slowly turns the graded test paper over. Her heart sinks—67%. "That test was unfair," she says to a neighboring student sporting an A+ grade. When the teacher goes over the test, Shelby defiantly challenges every one of her wrong answers: "Why is that wrong? Why isn't my answer right?" she whines. Later, when the teacher presents new material, Shelby sits sideways in her chair with notebook closed, arms folded across her chest, and steam pouring from her ears. Shelby's oppositional posture lets the teacher know that Shelby's bad test performance is the teacher's fault. Of course, it's not. Shelby's lackluster performance is because of her own inadequate study behaviors, such as incomplete note taking, reread-ing, and rehearsal. And Shelby's brooding and blaming are not going to fix the problem. Shelby must shift the blame from the teacher to herself if she is to raise achievement.

In summary, goal seekers need to remain focused despite the obstacles that arise. President Woodrow Wilson said, "You should nurse your dreams and protect them through the bad times and tough times to the sunshine and light that always come." Overcoming obstacles, though, depends on attributing success or failure to one's own actions rather than nonfactors, like luck and genetics. When it comes to blaming bad situa-tions for one's mistakes and failures, consider what employment guru Robert Half said, "The search for blame is always successful." Elaine Maxwell, education consultant, sums focus up best:

> My will shall shape my future. Whether I fail or succeed shall be no one's doing but my own. I am the force; I can clear any obstacle before me or be lost in the maze. My choice; my responsibility; win or lose, only I hold the key to my destiny.

Using the DIFS Will Riser to Boost Focus

Ms. Perkins uses the DIFS Will Riser shown in Exhibit 6.1 to boost Troy's focus. Together they set a launch date for blasting off to better health and higher health class achievement. Ms. Perkins demonstrates how Troy can use the time line matrix (Exhibit 6.4) to record his daily exercise, diet, and study time progress. Finally, Ms. Perkins and Troy address and counter potential obstacles Troy believes might block his progress, such as limited time, a family history leaning toward obesity, and self-doubt that he is smart enough to excel academically.

SUSTAIN

Let me tell you the secret that led to my goal. My strength lies solely in my tenacity.

—Louis Pasteur

Getting there is only half the battle. Change is hard; sustaining change is even harder (see Prochaska et al., 2002). Consider those who changed and now strive to sustain a life without smoking or drinking. It's easy to slip back to old ways. Perhaps you've heard these sayings: "You're just a puff away from a pack" and "One drink, one drunk."

Motivation must be sustained. Exercise or diet programs that start and stop more often than a New York City cab won't take you where you want to go. Most people find it difficult to sustain motivation. When it comes to fulfilling New Years' resolutions, for example, most fall lightly like confetti. Eighty percent are eventually broken, and one third don't last a month (Parker-Pope, 2007). It's hard to adhere to the best of ideas.

But sustaining motivation produces remarkable results. Remember that the tortoise persevered and clipped the hare at the tape. A tiny trickle of water over a million years moves mountains more than an upstart earthquake. And thousands of years of evolution transformed apes into humans—except for your uncle with the really hairy knuckles. Speaking of humans, what about pitching ace Nolan Ryan who was still throwing smoke well into his 40s while his contemporaries were selling used cars and lobbing pitches at Old-Timers games. Ryan attributed longevity to sustaining a rigorous workout regiment.

Similarly, students who plug away—registering small gains—throughout the school year and their academic career are likely to accomplish a great deal. My former graduate adviser at Florida State University offered a simple piece of advice each time he met with a student: "Stay with it now." What a great piece of advice. It means that no matter how difficult or impossible things seem, you just stay with it, keep plugging away, and never give up.

Sustained motivation is likely when two things happen: Behavior is rewarded, and a supportive lifestyle change is adopted. We look at these in turn.

Rewards

Think back to desire—the D in DIFS. Desire stems from the pursuit of some reward. The reward can be something tangible, such as high grades or trophies, or something more spiritual, such as the joy of learning or the love of the game. Although pursuing rewards fuels desire, gaining rewards sustains focus. Without some reward, change is transitory rather than sustained. Remember, too, that the best rewards are the more spiritual, internal ones. Tangible rewards eventually lose their luster, but passion is difficult to tarnish. I've been a runner for 30 years because I enjoy running. No trophy could sustain such a long track record. Sort of speaking about long treks, I have a friend who works as a guide at Rocky Mountain National Park, leading families on long, wilderness hikes six days a week. On her single day off, you might imagine that she sleeps in, soaks her bunions, and puts her feet up. Nope, she hikes. It's what she loves to do. That passion has helped her scale many mountains over many years.

Lifestyle Change

Remember earlier in the chapter, there was a woman who wanted to increase fitness by developing an exercise program but also wanted to maintain a lifestyle—of smoking, drinking, and late nights—at odds with fitness. That approach won't fly for long; opposing forces cannot be sustained. The woman needs to drop the fitness drainers. But here is the clincher: She needs to do more than remove old habits; she needs to begin new ones consistent with a fitness lifestyle (Prochaska et al., 2002). To sustain her exercise program, she must lead a supportive fitness life. She'll probably monitor her weight, eat healthy foods, take multivitamins, drink plenty of water, read health magazines, wear spandex tights, and stretch while waiting on line at the grocery store. To sustain fitness, the woman will replace old, bad habits with new, good ones. And as author Colleen Mariah Rae said, "Good habits" (once developed) "are just as hard to break as bad ones."

Using the DIFS Will Riser to Boost Sustainment

Ms. Perkins uses the DIFS Will Riser shown in Exhibit 6.1 to boost Troy's sustained work toward his goals. She showcases the rewards he's earned by sending him weekly letters touting his accomplishments related to study time, course grade, exercise, and diet. She reminds him that the reward of attending the college basketball team's practice is in site. She also directs Troy to recognize internal gains, such as how much better he feels, looks, and plays basketball, because of his health change behaviors. Ms. Perkins also reminds Troy that certain lifestyle changes are probably needed to sustain goal progress. She points out that eating fast food three or four times a week and sleeping just seven hours a night are lifestyle patterns incompatible with good health and in need of change.

STRATEGY INSTRUCTION: TEACHING STUDENTS TO MOTIVATE

Here is an example of goal statement strategy instruction for a high school band.

> "Okay, band members, our school band has a long, distinguished legacy of success. To keep pace, we need to be highly motivated, and motivation begins with setting goals. Today, with your help, I'd like to set some goals for our band. Tonight, you should use the same goal-setting strategy I model and set your personal music goals for the year." (*Introduce and sell the strategy*)
>
> "It's important that goals meet certain characteristics. They should be challenging rather than easy. Challenging goals make you work harder and achieve more. Perhaps you've heard the expression, 'No one rises to low expectations.' Goals should be long range and short range. It's best to first set long-range goals and then specify the short-range goals that can get us there. Finally, goals should be made public, so that others hold us to our goals and lend help along the way. Let's get started." (*Introduce and sell the strategy*)
>
> "I believe we should have three long-range goals. The first is to win the annual Battle of the Marching Bands competition this fall. The second is that our symphonic band earns an A+ in the winter music competition. Last, we should master and perform the most difficult piece of music ever attempted by a high school band: Aaron Copeland's *El Salon Mexico*." I've written these on the board. (*Introduce the strategy*)

Long-Range Goals	Win Battle of Marching Bands	Attain A+ Competition Grade	Master *El Salon Mexico*
Short-Range Goals	Learn and perfect 4 routines Improve turns and rearbacks	Learn and perfect 5 compositions Improve instrument balance	Improve tone quality Improve dynamics

"These goals are certainly challenging and measurable. We can publicize our goals in a story in the school paper and by telling family and friends. We'll also post our goals in the band room. That way, we'll see them every time we rehearse. We'll also make cards with these goal statements that you can post on your music stands at home and inside your instrument cases." (*Introduce the strategy*)

"As for short-range goals that can help us meet our long-range goals, say what a few of those might be and I'll write them on the board." (*Perfect the strategy*)

"Goal statements work well in all areas. I've used them in golf for years. This year my goal is to break 100—for nine holes. I've also set goals for saving for retirement and for a new car to replace that rusty beater in the parking lot. You should practice using the goal-setting strategy by designating some of your own long- and short-range goals. Remember to make them challenging and to devise a plan for publicizing them." (*Perfect and generalize the strategy*)

7

Helping Students Manage Behavior

We want students to soar to success, but sometimes they're grounded—doing things they are not supposed to do. During a math lesson, students might talk to other students, fiddle with their calculators, thumb through their literature book, doodle on their sneakers, get a drink of water, or think about their lunch plans. Although these are minor offenses, they disrupt learning nonetheless.

Classroom discipline has long been considered the most serious problem facing our nation's schools (Evertson & Weinstein, 2006). In fact, teachers commonly lose about half of their instructional time dealing with discipline problems and disruptive behavior; each student is off task about two and one-half times every minute (Cotton, 1990). Here is the good news: This chapter describes preventive, surface, and control strategies teachers can employ to strengthen classroom behavior. Moreover, it equips teachers to teach students how to manage their own behavior. Only when behavior is properly managed can students soar to success.

PREVENTIVE STRATEGIES

You've heard the expression, "The best defense is a good offense." It means that if your team has the ball, the other team cannot score. The same is true with classroom management. If you get students to do the right thing, then you need not stop inappropriate behavior. Ideally, teachers want a smooth, well functioning classroom where off-task behaviors rarely occur. Four methods for preventing off-task behavior are described.

Arrange the Environment for Success

Years ago, I attended the U.S. Elementary School Chess Championship. Thousands of scholastic players from across the United States participated in the three-day tournament vying for the overall championship or other class prizes. For this important mind taxing event, you would expect ideal playing conditions where players can fully concentrate as they ponder and calculate their moves. That was hardly the case. Instead, players were crammed into a hotel meeting room that was too small. Eight players competed at playing tables better suited for four players. Limited spacing between table rows also offered little room for players to maneuver when they got up to stretch their legs. Chairs collided with those alongside or behind them. When players frequently ventured into the tiny center or side aisles, these were mobbed with other players and spectators. One small open doorway in and out of the room was also crammed while roughly 60 people pushed their way through every minute. The doorway led to an open area where players and spectators gathered and talked boisterously just outside the tournament room. You get the picture. The movement, noise, and limited space made it difficult to play one's best chess. This was a poorly engineered environment.

I tell this story because I routinely observe poorly engineered schools and classrooms that hinder learning. Recently, I visited a school where two classrooms were separated by a floor to ceiling partition—which was left wide open. The noise generated by the two classes made it difficult to hear the teacher or concentrate on seatwork. Moreover, students' attention was often stolen by what was happening in the other classroom. Recall from Chapter 2 my own classroom where students dragged and clanged their chairs and carted materials from their desks to meet in reading groups. This daily disruption was squelched through better engineering: assembling a carpeted and furnished reading center that muted sound and eliminated furniture transportation.

Although teachers struggling with bad classroom environments probably cannot expand classroom dimensions or erect walls, they can engineer a productive learning environment. They can begin by arranging furniture or students in ways that promote learning and limit distractions. One key way is moving students closer to instruction. When I teach chess in elementary classrooms, I move students from their desks, which are spread about the room, to an area where all students can sit comfortably on the floor in close proximity to me and a chess demonstration board. Similarly, when I teach 125 college students in a cavernous lecture hall, I require that students fill in the rows closer to the front before taking residence in a seat further back. In both instances, I want students in close proximity to instruction where it is easier for them to maintain attention and easier for me to monitor their learning and behavior.

Here are other engineering tips to prevent distractions. Regulate the thermostat so that students are comfortable. Close partitions and doors to block out noises. Adjust the blinds to prevent glare or to shield students from outside distractions, such as cars and games of foursquare. Arrange for adequate storage, so that students are not distracted by coats, backpacks, books, and other supplies in their work area. Remove or move things not relevant to instruction that might distract students, such as class pets, posters, or old information written on the board. Turn off computer screens and televisions not in use.

Establish Effective Rules and Routines

Although it's not difficult to establish a long list of classroom rules that cover virtually everything from a to z, such as "*atrocities* committed against substitute teachers" to "the proper care and treatment of *zoo* animals encountered on field trips," I recommend against doing so. First of all, such lists are hardly foolproof. When confronted with a lot of rules, people naturally seek loopholes. Another problem is that most rule lists are negative; they tell students what they can't do rather than what they can do.

I present students (whether working with kindergartners or graduate students) with a single positive rule: Be a good student. That's it. I tell them,

> There is just one rule in this classroom: Be a good student. You know what good students do; they are on-task, doing what they are supposed to be doing. If you are supposed to be listening intently, then do that; working quietly and independently, then do that; contributing constructively and politely to a class discussion, then do that. Be a good student at all times; do what you are supposed to do.

Of course, this one-rule approach depends on making clear what students are to do. And effective classroom managers do just that; they specify what is expected in behavioral terms. "Get busy" is a vague instruction compared to, "Complete the first five math problems on page 26." The directive "pay attention" is less instructive than "turn your body toward me, place your pencil inside your desk, and listen to how communism and capitalism are alike and different." Of course, established routines are best for guiding and preserving good student behavior.

Poorly conceived routines sabotage classroom behavior. Here's one:

> Okay, kids, you've been out of control all morning and I've had enough! I'm writing letter spaces for two words on the

board. . . . All right, stop calling out letters. No, Ferris, you can't buy a vowel. Amanda, please sit down. I don't want you to be Vanna White. . . . Okay, where was I? Oh yeah, the letter spaces are for the words "no recess." Each time anyone misbehaves, I'm filling in one of the eight letters. If I write "no recess" before lunch time, there is no recess.

This routine won't work because it actually encourages students to misbehave seven more times—well, actually eight. Students can misbehave seven times before reaching the fatal, final letter *s* in recess. And if they misbehave one more time after that, the teacher is likely to give them yet another chance: "That behavior is unacceptable too. I'm writing down *part* of the final *s*." After all, the teacher really doesn't want to miss recess either.

Some misguided routines are deflating. Some teachers still assemble teams for athletic or academic contests by designating student captains and having them alternate team picks—a cruel, public elimination process that exposes and humiliates the weak. One of my former teachers returned tests in a publicly embarrassing way before student privacy rights were established. "Okay boys and girls, I graded your science tests and will return them to you now. I need all students to rise from their seats and stand along the side wall. Okay, Alice had the best score, a 98. Alice, you now sit in the first seat in the front row. Charles, nice work, 95, please sit next to Alice. And so it went; one by one, until all scores were announced publicly and all students were reseated from front to back according to their descending test scores. As I recollect, things often finished up something like this: "And finally, Mr. Kiewra, you managed a 57. Oh, it looks like we're out of chairs. Perhaps you can go next door and ask to borrow one."

Teachers should establish effective routines for matters as mundane as pencil sharpening to those as important as test taking. The "Rrrrrrr, Rrrrrrr, Rrrrrrr" of a pencil sharpener distracts teachers and students. Free access to the pencil sharpener during instruction or work time is a poor routine. A better routine limits pencil sharpening to designated times, such as before class or during breaks. Students in dire need of a sharpened pencil can borrow one from a public can of sharpened pencils or can use a personal sharpener at their desk.

Teachers should establish effective testing routines that place students at ease, limit distractions, and derail cheating. Here are some of my test-taking routines:

- Students sit a seat apart whenever possible.
- All books and personal materials are placed below one's seat.
- Alternate forms of the test are distributed to adjacent students.
- General instructions are announced before students begin the test.

- Students must shield test booklets and answer sheets so they cannot be seen by others.
- Students who have questions raise their hands and the teacher comes to them.

Be "With-It" and Smooth

Although you know the drummer for the band 50 Cent and can order the perfect wine to complement any entrée, those talents do not necessarily make you "with-it" or "smooth" according to Jacob Kounin (1970), who discovered nearly 40 years ago that these two factors are related to effective classroom management. He found that students are better behaved and learn more when teachers are with-it and smooth than when they are not.

According to Kounin (1970), with-it teachers are aware of what's happening throughout the classroom. Like Santa Claus, they know who is sleeping, who is awake, and who is bad or good. With-it teachers have eyes in the back of their head. Nothing escapes them. Moreover, with-it teachers foresee and offset oncoming problems. They nip potential problems in the bud.

Some teachers are far from with-it. My junior high English teacher was nicknamed Mrs. Oblivious, because she was unaware that students flung a resin bag around the room, even though walls and students were caked in the white powdery substance, or that students tossed increasingly larger objects out the window—pencils, books, chairs, and eventually Sean Handley. My high school science teacher was unaware that students escaped from his classroom by creeping on the floor through a rear door to a science preparation room with access to the hallway and freedom. In another class, students actually grilled meat on a George Foreman grill inside the classroom without the teacher noticing. Perhaps, the smoke was too thick to see what was happening!

On the other end of the with-it continuum are teachers like Mr. Goldman, an imposing figure who resembled the Hulk—only greener. Students were angels in his class, not because of his stature or monster green hue, but because he was on top of things—with-it. He had the eyes of a hawk. From across the room, he saw if you were on the right page, if your homework was completed, if a written answer was correct, and if a field mouse skittered across the floor. He picked up sound—even faint whispers—better than an FBI wiretap. And he sensed things before they even happened. When a student started to drift off, Mr. Goldman appeared alarmingly at his side. A student about to talk to another student was "interrupted" by a Mr. Goldman question. Mr. Goldman even handed one surprised student a box of tissues even though the student had not sneezed or asked for tissues. Seconds later, the student sneezed.

According to Kounin (1970), effective classroom managers are also smooth as they keep students engaged and instructional momentum flowing. I once attended a national conference where a distinguished presenter was speaking to about 500 people. After describing his research methods, he moved to the overhead projector and flipped the switch to reveal his results. The projector bulb flickered, popped, and went black. Without missing a beat, the presenter picked up the tiny transparency crammed with numbers, held it aloft, and said, "As you can see, these are light popping results." The crowd laughed and then listened intently as the presenter simply described the findings. Rather than let failed technology grind the presentation to a halt, the presenter made a smooth recovery. Smooth teachers share three characteristics: good pacing and transitions, group focus, and an ability to overlap.

When instruction is too fast, students' brains lag behind and strain to catch up. Teachers who quickly rattle off a string of terms and definitions exceed students' capacity to listen, take notes, and learn. When instruction is too slow, students' brains move off task and contemplate other things. Teachers sometimes slow down instruction using poor routines. For example, a science teacher might instruct students, one row at a time, to "add the blue solution to the mixture," rather than have all students do this at the same time. Poor instructional pace hinders learning. Effective instructors keep a lively pace and adjust the instructional pace as needed in order to keep students engaged.

Rough transitions can also sabotage a lesson. Teachers sometimes thrust students into a new activity or lesson before they are ready. For instance, a teacher begins a lesson on writing style while students returning from recess are still getting drinks, sharpening pencils, or rifling through their desk looking for their writing folder. Teachers sometimes interrupt their own lessons. A teacher speaking about European history might suddenly remember the impending class trip to the museum and ask, "Who still needs to bring in a permission slip for our field trip?" Avoid unnecessary slowdowns and jerky transitions that halt instructional momentum.

Smoothness also hinges on teachers maintaining a group focus. Smooth teachers keep all students on their toes. Rather than call on students in some predictable order—allowing students to drift off task when their turn is past or in the distant future—smooth teachers maintain a group focus by calling on students randomly or by having all students respond in unison—either orally, with a show of hands, or in writing. When a student goes to the board to write an answer, there are no spectators. Other students work the problem at their desks. When a student poses a question or offers a comment, the smooth teacher makes sure that the entire group focuses on the student's input by first asking another student in the class to respond.

Smooth teachers overlap their attention among multiple tasks. In today's vernacular, they multitask. For example, they keep the momentum of a language arts group flowing—"You've raised a question that deserves a thoughtful response; everyone write a solution"—before moving out into the classroom to help a student who needs assistance. While a class is working math problems, the smooth teacher seems to offer assistance and encouragement in several places at once. "Mandy, you're forgetting to carry," the teacher says while catching Ben's eye and nodding to let Ben know she'll be there next. On her way to help Ben, the teacher quickly offers direction to Brad, "Brad, wrap up problems 7 through 10 now and then raise your hand for me to check them," and encouragement to Patti, "This looks good, Patti; keep it going."

SURFACE STRATEGIES

You've met Mrs. Oblivious, whose students flung a resin bag around the classroom and tossed objects out the window, and Mr. Goldman, a greenish but very with-it teacher, whose students behaved like angels. You might be surprised to learn that the devilish students in Mrs. Oblivious's class and the angelic students in Mr. Goldman's class were the same students. Everyday, the same group of students had English with Mrs. Oblivious and then had social studies with Mr. Goldman. This puzzling situation reveals that students are not inherently good or bad. Rather, student behavior is a function of the environment. Student behavior changes, sometimes drastically, depending on the setting. Think about it. You don't behave the same way in all settings. In church, you act church. At work, you act work. And in a buffet line, you act like a bear preparing to hibernate.

When students are off task, the root of the problem lies on the surface—within the immediate classroom environment—rather than below the surface (see Charles, 1992, chap. 3). Too often, however, teachers blame off-task behavior on subterranean factors that have no bearing and cannot be controlled, anyway. For example, when Susie misbehaves at the start of math, the teacher attributes Susie's behavior to her parents impending divorce. When, Johnny neglects to complete his homework, the teacher lets it go because Johnny comes from a poor family that probably does not have the time or inclination to help him. And when Tara is annoying Amy throughout a science lecture, the teacher chalks it up to Tara's low self-image. Given these deep-rooted reasons for off-task behavior, the teacher is virtually helpless to improve classroom behavior. The only recourse is to play matchmaker and reunite Susie's parents, donate a large sum of money to Johnny's family to raise their standard of living, and begin a program of therapy to boost Tara's self-image. Thank goodness, Paul has remained on task while his family searches desperately to find a kidney donor for his uncle.

But the problems and solutions, of course, lie on the surface. And that surface can usually be soiled or wiped clean by the teacher. Susie was on task just moments ago when wrapping up English. Why didn't the impending divorce pull her off task then? The reason is that Susie is successful in English and struggles in math. Susie's misbehavior in math is a reaction to that struggle. Her misbehavior occurred when she attempted math problems that were too difficult for her. The teacher can get Susie back on task immediately by providing math assistance or assigning math problems more at her level. Yes, Johnny's family is poor, but Johnny chooses not to complete his homework because the teacher lets him get away with not doing it. The teacher is probably not aware that Johnny practices his band instrument every day at home because the band teacher expects and rewards daily practice—even for children from poor families. The classroom teacher can bolster Johnny's homework output by rewarding him for completed assignments. And Tara's annoying behavior toward Amy throughout science is not because of a low self-image but because Tara does not get along with Amy. Tara behaves fine when sitting near other students. There is no need for the teacher to fix Tara's self-image or even her relationship with Amy. The teacher need only separate the students.

Teachers need to focus on the immediate environment. At 9:00 in the morning, when off-task behavior occurs in the classroom, teachers cannot dwell on outside factors such as divorce, socioeconomic status, self-image, intelligence, gender, or race. A teacher's job begins where these outside factors leave off. This is not to say that things such as family, self image, race, and gender are unimportant. They are important. But they are not the immediate causes or solutions to the problems that arise at 9:00 a.m. The problems and solutions lie along the top surface of the classroom environment.

When off-task behavior occurs, teachers must determine what surface factor is responsible and what surface technique might quickly and subtly get the student back on task. The technique must work quickly so that a ripple effect (Kounin, 1970) does not occur. A ripple effect occurs when a deviant behavior spreads among students throughout the classroom. For example, a student leaves his seat to get a drink of water during a science lesson. If this behavior goes unchecked, then several students might soon do the same. Or a student groans when the teacher assigns class work causing other students to laugh. If the groaning behavior goes unchecked, then other students will likely join the chorus.

A surface technique is best applied subtly. Teachers should not draw undo attention to the deviant behavior. Drawing attention to the deviant behavior shifts the class's attention from the task at hand to the deviant behavior. Then, all students are off task. Suppose you are presenting a lesson to the class and notice that Melinda, seated at the back of the classroom, leans over and whispers something to Jennifer. Here's what *not* to do: "Melinda, what are you doing talking during class? Not only are you not paying attention, you are disturbing Jennifer." That surface technique is hardly subtle. It pulls the entire class and the teacher off task. The teacher has made a mountain out of a mole hill. So how should a teacher handle Melinda's whisper? Assuming that Melinda's whispering is not a chronic problem, ignore it. It is likely an isolated incident. Moreover, there is little chance for a ripple effect because the whispering was unnoticed by others. If the whispering persists, several surface techniques might work. The teacher can catch Melinda's eye, walk toward her, raise an index finger to her lips, or ask Melinda a question about the lesson. In each case, Melinda's off-task behavior is handled subtly without pulling others off task.

Proximity Control, Signals, and Lesson Hurdling

Proximity control, signals, and lesson hurdling are three effective surface techniques that teachers use to quickly and subtly help students get back on task (Charles, 1992). When a student is off task, the teacher can control the behavior by moving in close proximity to that student. Few students remain off task when the teacher hovers nearby. Be smooth when using proximity control. Maintain the momentum of the lesson as you move subtly toward the off-task student. Also, do not become anchored to a podium or piece of technology when you teach. Using proximity control requires you to sometimes circulate throughout the classroom and teach from different spots.

Sometimes, it is difficult to move in close proximity to students. I teach 125 students in a cavernous lecture hall and cannot easily move next to students in the rear of the classroom or along the sidewalls. Fortunately, I can send long-range signals to students who are off task in order to get them back on task. It all begins with eye contact. A student who is not looking at you cannot receive your signal. To establish eye contact, continue to look toward the student until contact is made. Should the student be looking elsewhere, you can likely gain the student's attention by simply pausing (nothing grabs attention like silence), varying your voice volume or cadence, or providing some other attention cue, such as a clap or a tap on the desk. Once eye contact is established, that is often enough to curtail an off-task behavior. If not, provide a more overt signal such as raised eyebrows, a prolonged stare, a cocked head, a frown, or a raised hand. In my 25 years of teaching, I have probably overtly asked a student to stop an off-task behavior fewer than 10 times. Instead, I strive to create an environment where off-task behavior is unlikely to occur. When it does occur, I employ surface techniques such as proximity control and signals that get student behavior back on track.

Oftentimes, off-task behaviors occur when students struggle with assignments. They become confused by directions or frustrated by their limited progress. Rather than seek help, confused or frustrated students might display off-task behaviors such as talking, daydreaming, doodling, or wandering around the room. In such instances, students need help hurdling the lesson. Students might need clarification of instructions ("In each sentence you are supposed to underline the verb phrase and circle the verb marker."), remediation ("The verb marker is a verb helper. In the sentence 'They are talking,' *talking* is the main verb and *are* is the verb marker."), a simple hint ("As you work this problem, remember that the verb marker always precedes the main verb but there might be other words between them."), or reassurance ("This is looking really good; you have a strong grasp of verb markers."). Another hurdle helper is reducing the number of problems a student must attempt. Some students become overwhelmed and sent off task by an abundance of problems. Must students work 20 long division problems, for example, when just 10 problems provide ample practice and can reveal competence level and error patterns? You know from your own experience that overwhelming tasks such as cleaning an entire house yield more off-task behaviors than cleaning a single room.

CONTROL STRATEGIES

Is it ethical to control behavior? It is not only ethical to control behavior; it is a teacher's job. Teachers must help students produce appropriate academic and social behaviors and limit inappropriate ones. Psychologists have discovered certain strategies that control behavior (Skinner, 1953; Sulzer-Azaroff & Mayer, 1977). Four of them are covered in this section. One of them, reinforcement, strengthens desired behaviors. The other three—punishment, extinction, and time-out—decrease unwanted behaviors. Exhibit 7.1 displays these strategies.

Reinforcement

Reinforcement strengthens behavior. Therefore, it should be used following a desired behavior so that the desired behavior occurs more frequently. Most of the time, students are on task, doing what they are supposed to be doing. Teachers need to catch students doing the right things and reinforce those behaviors so that they occur more often.

Exhibit 7.1 shows the two types of reinforcement: positive and negative. Although both strengthen behavior, positive reinforcement involves the presentation of a stimulus following a behavior, whereas negative reinforcement

EXHIBIT 7.1   Control Strategies

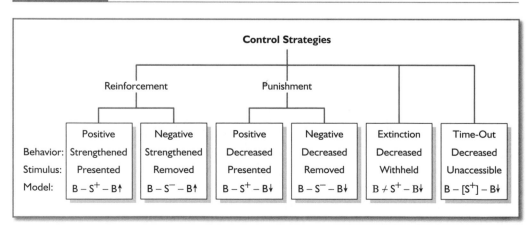

	Reinforcement		Punishment			
	Positive	Negative	Positive	Negative	Extinction	Time-Out
Behavior:	Strengthened	Strengthened	Decreased	Decreased	Decreased	Decreased
Stimulus:	Presented	Removed	Presented	Removed	Withheld	Unaccessible
Model:	$B - S^+ - B\uparrow$	$B - S^- - B\uparrow$	$B - S^+ - B\downarrow$	$B - S^- - B\downarrow$	$B \nrightarrow S^+ - B\downarrow$	$B - [S^+] - B\downarrow$

involves the removal of a stimulus following a behavior. As an example of positive reinforcement, Marty writes a good book report (the behavior), receives a high grade from his teacher (a presented stimulus), and, consequently, turns in good book reports on subsequent assignments (a strengthening of the behavior). As an example of negative reinforcement, Marcy is told by her teacher that she must write two additional book reports for this assignment if her book report is not good. Marcy writes a good book report (the behavior), avoids the teacher's threat of writing additional book reports (the removal of a stimulus), and, consequently, turns in good book reports on subsequent assignments (a strengthening of the behavior).

Because of reinforcement, Marty and Marcy each write good book reports. However, Marty works to earn something favorable (good grades), whereas Marcy works to avoid something aversive (extra report writing). As another example of how positive and negative reinforcement compare, examine the illustration in Exhibit 7.2. Notice that one horse runs fast to get the carrot (positive reinforcement) while the other runs fast to remove the threat of a whipping (negative reinforcement). Both techniques work, but examine the horses' expressions. The horse chasing the carrot is happy; the horse avoiding the whip is distraught. When positive reinforcement is used in school, students strive to earn positive rewards such as praise, high grades, smiley faces, and self-satisfaction. When negative reinforcement is used, students strive to avoid negative consequences such as low grades, extra work, and embarrassment. I strongly recommend that positive reinforcement be used over negative reinforcement.

EXHIBIT 7.2   Illustration Showing Positive Versus Negative Reinforcement

Positive reinforcement should be ongoing as you catch kids doing the right thing throughout the school day ("Nice job on the spelling assignment, Keaton. . . . I appreciate you raising your hand, Anna. . . . Sam, thanks for helping your group members. . . ."). Teachers can even get other students in on the positive reinforcement act. One teacher I know invented several clever clapping methods (try saying that three times fast) for students to use when they recognize and reward a student's behavior. The "round of applause" clap is done with the hands moving in a circular motion. The "ketchup bottle" clap mimics a fist tapping the bottom of a stubborn ketchup bottle. And the "sprinkler" clap imitates a pulsating sprinkler. In addition to using positive reinforcement spontaneously throughout the day, teachers might consider using any of three positive reinforcement programs: token economy, Premack principle, and shaping.

In token economies (Hundert, 1976), the presented stimulus, the reinforcer, is a token. A token can be a poker chip or some other tangible object. The token is like money. It has no inherent value of its own, but it can be redeemed for other reinforcers of choice. During my college days, I had a teaching experience at a "camp" for teenage boys who had broken the law. They lived at the camp, rather than in jail, and were educated there. The camp used a token economy to motivate the campers. Tokens were awarded for all sorts of positive behaviors from completing homework to releasing hostages. Later, the campers redeemed their tokens for more valued reinforcers such as extra recreation time, snack food, and weapons. Of course, I'm kidding about some of this, but you get the point that the campers were motivated to earn tokens and redeem them for valued items. The token economy produced a lot of positive behavior and happy campers.

Guess who invented the Premack principle. I'll give you a hint: Who's buried in Grant's tomb? Give up? It was Grant, of course. Now, who do you think invented the Premack principle? No, it's not Grant! Ugh! Anyway, it was George Premack (1959) who developed the following principle: A preferred activity can be used to positively reinforce a nonpreferred activity. Eating lima beans is a nonpreferred activity for most children, whereas eating chocolate cake is generally a preferred activity. A parent using the Premack principle might say, "Eat your lima beans and then you can eat cake." A teacher using the principle might say, "Complete your math problems quietly and correctly (a low-preference activity), and then we can go outside for recess (a high-preference activity)" or "Let's tidy the classroom (low preference); then I'll read you another chapter of *The Lion, the Witch, and the Wardrobe*" (high preference).

Shaping involves positively reinforcing successively closer approximations of a target behavior. I saw a movie where behavioral psychologist B. F. Skinner used shaping to make a pigeon turn around in a counterclockwise direction. The pigeon was placed in a box that contained a food tray that opened at the front of the box anytime Skinner pressed a button. The pigeon was positioned in the box facing forward. Skinner watched the pigeon and waited for it to make a slight counterclockwise turn. As soon as that happened, Skinner pressed the button that released the food tray, which contained a pellet that the pigeon immediately consumed. Skinner then waited for the pigeon to make a counterclockwise turn slightly larger than the first. When that happened, the bird was again fed. Skinner continued to reinforce the bird with food pellets each time it turned more counterclockwise than the time before. Within minutes, the pigeon was turning circles faster than an Olympic skater.

In academic circles, shaping might be used to shape handwriting. A child's initial printing of the letter A is reinforced, even though it barely resembles the target letter ("Oh, look at that, you made an A"). Over time, the child receives reinforcement each time a successive attempt to print letter A is better than the previously reinforced attempt ("Oh, wow, your printing is really improving"). Of course, most children are smarter than pigeons, so they can also benefit from other techniques mixed with shaping such as modeling ("Watch how I begin printing the letter") and lesson hurdles ("Try to make that line go straight across").

Punishment

When you hear the word *punishment*, what comes to mind? Many people conjure up harsh images of spankings, dunce caps, and incarcerations. These bleak but popular images give punishment a bad name. Few people imagine punishment delivered in these milder forms: a slight shake of the head, a glance, the removal of a token, the reduction of points, or the comments "please return to your seat" and "no, the answer is seven." All of these things might serve as punishers. As shown in Exhibit 7.1, punishment occurs any time a behavior decreases following the presentation of a stimulus (positive punishment) or the removal of a stimulus (negative punishment). For example, if Sonja is out of her seat (a behavior), and the teacher says "please return to your seat" (a presented stimulus), and Sonja returns to her seat (a decrease in out-of-seat behavior), then positive punishment has occurred. If Leon says "4 + 3 = 6" (a behavior), and the teacher says "no, the answer is seven" (a presented stimulus), and Leon no longer says that 4 + 3 = 6 (a decrease in incorrectly stating an addition fact), then positive punishment has occurred. Here are two examples of negative punishment: (1) Marisa arrives late for class (a behavior), the teacher fines Marisa a token for being late (removal of a stimulus), and Marisa is not late thereafter (a decrease in behavior); (2) Stephen's writing assignment is sloppy (a behavior), the teacher deducts five points from Stephen's grade (removal of a stimulus), and Stephen no longer turns in sloppy papers (a decrease in behavior). You can see from these examples that punishment need not be a dirty word or a horrifying experience. Any stimulus presentation or removal that decreases behavior qualifies as punishment. Certainly, mild and judicious punishment has a place in school when teachers seek to decrease inappropriate behavior.

When administering punishment, be sure the punishment is intense enough to decrease behavior. There's an old story about a dog lying on a porch moaning and groaning alongside his owner. A passerby asks the owner why the dog is moaning and groaning. "He's lying on a nail," the owner flatly responds. "Why doesn't he get off then?" the passerby asks. "Because it doesn't hurt him bad enough," the owner answers. Oftentimes, we, like the dog, receive a mild form of punishment that might lead us to moan and groan but not really change our behavior. I once drove a car that made a small grinding sound when I shifted the car into second gear. When I told my father this, he remarked that there are no such things as small grinding sounds or small explosions. Anyway, although the grinding noise drove me a little crazy, it was not bothersome enough to drive me into the hands of an expensive mechanic. You get the point; punishment must be intense enough to work.

Some teachers, you'll notice, are constantly shushing their students. But the students keep right on talking out of turn, because the shushing is too mild a punisher. Some teachers put a checkmark in their grade book each time a student misses a homework assignment. The checks are intended to punish students for missed homework and reduce that behavior. If the checks, however, have little or no bearing on students' course grades, they continue to miss homework assignments. The checkmark "punishers" have no real bite. When you use punishment, make the punishment intense enough to reduce the target behavior.

Extinction

It's break time. You head over to your favorite vending machine and slip in a dollar bill expecting to receive your favorite snack food. Nothing happens. You glare at the machine, and then give it a little shove. Still nothing happens. Reluctantly, you slide in another bill, say a short prayer, and make your selection. The machine stands motionless. You shove it and kick it. When it doesn't flinch, you stomp off refusing to feed it another dollar. The machine has extinguished your dollar-feeding behavior. As you can see in Exhibit 7.1, extinction occurs when reinforcement is withheld, making a previously reinforced behavior decrease. In the vending machine example, the withheld reinforcer is the snack. The previously reinforced behavior that is decreased is inserting money into the machine.

Here's another classic example of extinction. When an infant cries during the night, parents naturally comfort and feed it. Over time, the baby learns that crying (a behavior) bears food and comfort (reinforcers). When the time comes for the child to sleep through the night without food and comfort, parents must withhold reinforcement. This is not easy because the child has learned that he or she is supposed to cry at night, and the parents feel they are abandoning their child. Still, full extinction is the best method. In time, parents will no longer hear crying—when their child is off at college.

There is no shortage of opportunities for using extinction in school. When a student acts silly in class because doing so is historically reinforced by teacher attention, the teacher can withhold attention and reduce the silliness. A teacher who no longer wants to read sloppy papers can reduce sloppiness by withholding grades and comments from those papers. Sloppy papers are ignored. Extinction can also be used in combination with positive reinforcement. Extinction reduces an undesirable response, whereas positive reinforcement boosts a desirable one to take its place. A music teacher withholds comments when the student plays with a sour tone (extinction) and offers praise when the student plays with a melodic tone (positive reinforcement).

There are five considerations you should know about before using extinction in the classroom (Sulzer-Azaroff & Mayer, 1977, unit 11).

1. Watch out for a burst of behavior. When reinforcement is suddenly cut off, behavior does not decrease right away. In fact, it is likely to explode at first, while the person tries even harder to attain reinforcement. When extinction is first used to calm a tantruming student, the tantrum won't shut off like water from a faucet; it will gush before it drips.

2. Be consistent. Extinction takes time, because there is a history of reinforcement that must be reversed. The student who throws tantrums, for example, does so because that behavior is historically reinforced with teacher comfort. If extinction is applied, it might take several episodes before the student realizes that tantrums don't pay off anymore. Teachers must weather the storm and remain consistent.

3. Control the reinforcement source. Carter is behaving silly in class. As the teacher, you ignore the silliness and withhold the attention he seeks. You withhold reinforcement consistently, but the silly behavior persists. Here's the problem. Carter acts silly not to gain your attention but his classmates'. If they continue to smile and laugh, then Carter will continue acting silly. Teachers are not always the reinforcement source. In cases where reinforcement comes from students, extinction can still work, but the teacher must get the students to withhold reinforcement. In the Carter case, the teacher might tell students, "Class, when students act silly it disrupts class and it makes learning more difficult and time consuming. Here is what I'd like you to do. If a classmate acts silly, ignore it. When you do not smile or giggle at the silly behavior, the silly behavior will stop." The teacher can also add a dash of positive reinforcement to get students to comply: "If I notice you ignoring silly behavior, I'll be adding extra recess time."

4. Some behaviors are too dangerous to ignore. If two students begin to fight, now is not the time to try extinction. The same goes for chemistry students mishandling chemicals, children throwing sand in the sandbox, and physical education students snapping towels in the locker room. More immediate-working punishers are needed.

5. Watch out for modeling effects. "Monkey see, monkey do, monkey do the same as you." People, and especially children, imitate others. How else can you explain every student in America talking like this? "Uh, yeah, um, like, that is really cool, yeah, um, I'm down with it, Dude." When you use extinction you are allowing an inappropriate behavior to persist within full view of the class. It's possible that students will model the behavior, especially noticing that the behavior is going unpunished. The modeling effect might be softened by telling students you are choosing to ignore certain behaviors. Should the principal drop by to conduct a teacher observation, certainly discuss your extinction plan so the principal doesn't think you're oblivious to students squealing like monkeys.

Time-Out

If you've seen the show *Super Nanny*, then you're familiar with time-out. When children misbehave, Super Nanny often places them in time-out by having them sit in a designated place away from fun activities. As shown in Exhibit 7.1, time-out works to decrease inappropriate behavior by removing access to reinforcement. Suppose a preschool child is pulling books off a bookcase because she enjoys making a mess. A teacher can use time-out by removing the child from the bookcase—perhaps having her sit in a chair away from the bookcase—or can remove the bookcase from the area where the child is playing. In either case, the environment is changed so that access to reinforcement is removed.

Here are some other time-out examples in school settings:

- Suspending a student from school who has violated a school policy
- Having a student who is misbehaving on the playground stand off to the side and not participate
- Removing from a chess game a student who is insulting the opponent
- Turning off the computer of a student who is surfing the Web rather than typing a paper

Here are three important considerations for using time-out (Sulzer-Azaroff & Mayer, 1977):

1. Make the time-out setting aversive. The time-out setting should be uninteresting and certainly less reinforcing than the original setting. Suppose a student working at his or her seat is disruptive. The student is given time-out and sent to the back corner of the classroom. Once in that corner, the student is within reach of a computer, a stack of magazines, and the class marmoset. This is hardly an aversive environment. In fact, it is likely to be reinforcing. The inappropriate behavior that elicited the time-out process is likely to occur more frequently if reinforced in this way. A better time-out environment might be sitting in a chair facing a blank wall.

2. Do not make time-out too long. Usually 5 to 10 minutes is sufficient. When time-out is too long, students can adapt to the time-out situation, and it is no longer an aversive situation. Moreover, students might miss too much instruction. To minimize missed instruction, try to use time-out in ways that do not exclude students from instruction. A student can be moved to the rear of the classroom, away from a reinforcing environment, but face forward to follow instruction.

3. Do not use time-out to allow students to escape from "aversive" situations. Lydia hates physical education class and loathes exercise. When the P.E. teacher says, "It's calisthenics time," Lydia immediately begins hitting her classmates, prompting the teacher to put Lydia in time-out. But Lydia wins. She'd rather be in time-out than doing squat thrusts.

STRATEGY INSTRUCTION: TEACHING STUDENTS TO MANAGE BEHAVIOR

Just as teachers should teach students SOAR and motivational strategies, they should also teach students strategies for managing their own behavior. Self-management strategies are taught the same way that SOAR and motivation strategies are taught: Introduce, sell, perfect, and generalize the strategy all within the context of content instruction. Below is an example of strategy instruction aimed at improving time spent reading and, of course, self-mangement.

> "Tyler, you have not done enough reading outside of school—just 15 minutes per week. I'd like to see you raise that to 90 minutes per week. That's just 15 minutes per day, six days per week. I'll teach you a strategy so you can make this happen. I call the strategy Grandma's principle. A psychologist named Premack actually made this principle famous and named it after himself, but believe me—Grandmas were using this principle to change kids' behaviors long before psychology was invented. It works like this: You reward a low-preference behavior with a high-preference behavior. Grandmas, for instance, use the strategy to get grandkids to eat vegetables (a low-preference behavior) by promising a slice of Grandma's deluxe fudge brownie cake for dessert (a high-preference behavior) if vegetables are eaten. You can use this strategy to boost reading (a low-preference activity right now) by reading for at least 15 minutes and then rewarding yourself with 15 minutes of a high-preference activity, such as video games or playing outside." (*Introduce and sell the strategy*)
>
> "Let me show you how I use Grandma's principle to adhere to my nightly exercise routine. Exercise, for me, is a low-preference activity. Digital photography, however, is a high-preference activity.

So here is what I do. Every evening I ride my exercise bike for 20 minutes and then work on digital photography. Look at my monthly calendar where I record my exercise time and photography time each day." (*Introduce the strategy*)

"Tyler, I'd like you to practice Grandma's principle right now in class. Take out your reading book and read it for 10 minutes. When you are finished you can play a game on the computer for 10 minutes. Afterward, record your reading and play times in your daily planner." (*Perfect the strategy*)

"Grandma's principle, of course, can be used in almost any setting to increase a low-preference behavior. I also use it to reward house cleaning chores. After I knock off the laundry or clean the kitchen, I reward myself by reading a magazine. You can also use Grandma's principle to motivate yourself to complete other low-preference tasks such as cleaning your room or practicing the piano. And who knows, maybe you'll come to like reading and piano playing even more. I have to admit, I'm enjoying my nightly exercise more and more." (*Generalize the strategy*)

8

Helping Students Become Extraordinary

T his text has described ways to help students soar to success. For most readers, student success is characterized by high academic achievement, effective learning skills, and motivation to succeed. These are certainly challenging and important outcomes. But can students soar even higher?

Some people do extraordinary things—soar to amazing heights. Consider Mozart's musical compositions, Picasso's paintings, Freud's theory of the unconscious mind, Darwin's work on natural selection, Gandhi's social change movements, Crick and Watson's scientific discovery of DNA's double helix model, the Wright brothers' invention of the airplane, Martha Graham's dance movements, Virginia Woolf's introspective writings, Bobby Fischer's chess games, and Tiger Woods's golf shots.

How are such extraordinary contributions possible? Were these extraordinary creators born with talent, or was the talent largely made? And if talent is largely made, how do we make it? What roles can educators—teachers, coaches, and parents—play in making students extraordinary or at least more extraordinary?

IS TALENT BORN OR MADE?

At first glance, it looks like talent is born. Consider prodigies like Mozart, Picasso, and Fischer. Mozart (see Gardner, 1997) learned to play the piano at age 3. At 4, he taught himself to play the violin. At 5, he began to compose. Within two years, he composed regularly, toured Europe, and performed in leading concert halls. Picasso the child painted like an adult. American author Gertrude Stein said that young Picasso "wrote paintings as other children wrote their A, B, Cs" (Gardner, 1993, p. 140). When Bobby Fischer was 14, he became the youngest U.S. chess champion; he also soon became the youngest player in the world to attain the game's highest title—chess grandmaster.

Look more closely, though, and talent appears made even among these prodigies. Both Mozart and Picasso (Gardner, 1993) were born into their talent areas and jump-started by fathers well equipped to provide initial instruction in the talent domain. Mozart's father was a musician and composer; Picasso's father was an artist. Moreover, the duo's talents did not blossom for some time. Both worked at their crafts for many years before creating significant works. And they were hardly alone on the long road to talent development. Hayes (1985) studied outstanding composers and artists to determine the time interval between initial training and first significant contribution. Almost none of the extraordinary creators he studied developed significant works in less than 10 years—including the prodigious Mozart and Picasso. Mozart's first important composition was written when he was 16. Picasso was 25 when he painted his first significant work.

Bobby Fischer (see Brady, 1989) was not born into a chess family. Fischer worked hard at chess. He sat for hours at the board and thoughtfully played both sides of the game. He solved chess puzzles on his pocket set on the bus rides to and from school. Fischer voraciously read chess books and magazines, even those written in Russian—a language he taught himself because the best games and analyses appeared in Russian publications. Fischer even tucked chess literature inside his school books and studied chess under the guise of school learning. At lunch time, he ventured off campus to study chess with a local master. After school, he often frequented chess clubs in Brooklyn or Manhattan, where he learned at the feet of some of America's strongest grandmasters. He dropped out of school at 16 and pursued chess full time. Even with all this passion, practice, and mentorship, Fischer was not an overnight success. He did not win the world title until he was 29. Fischer's long climb to chess prominence was not unusual. Researchers studying chess grandmasters found that most only attain the grandmaster title after about 32,000 hours of intensive study (Charness, Krampe, & Mayr, 1996). Do the math: That's 11 years of study, 8 hours a day, 7 days a week. As was the case with musical composition and art, chess skills seem largely made, not born.

Most psychologists, though, adopt the stance that talent is part born and part made. Perhaps it's useful to think about talent like a rubber band. At birth, we all receive differing amounts of genetic potential, different sized rubber bands. Over the course of our lives, however, the bands can be stretched many times their size by environmental factors, such as instruction and practice, or the bands can hardly be stretched at all. The rubber band view is hopeful; talent is not fixed but modifiable, and environmental factors are the hands stretching the band.

Most psychologists also believe that our genetic potential, our rubber band, is best understood and measured in terms of general intelligence or IQ (see Gardner, 1997). Those with high IQ scores are destined to accomplish great things; those with low IQ scores are destined to struggle. It's not that simple. First, the correlation between intelligence and extraordinary talent is weak. High intelligence alone does not permit one to flourish in a domain (Gibson & Light, 1967). Highly gifted children with meteoric IQ scores generally carve out successful careers, but few ever make extraordinary contributions (Terman & Oden, 1947; see Wargo, 2006). As you'll soon learn, other factors such as passion and practice are more important than native intelligence. Second, IQ tests are limited in scope. They only measure verbal aptitude and logical reasoning—the kinds of skills valued in school. Although children with high IQs are well equipped to master school subjects steeped in language or logical reasoning, they are not necessarily equipped to master other areas such as music, art, or chess.

Harvard psychologist Howard Gardner (1993) believes there is not a unitary general intelligence but multiple intelligences—eight in all. In addition to linguistic and logical intelligences—the kinds measured on standard IQ tests—Gardner posits at least six other brands: musical, spatial, body kinesthetic, natural, interpersonal, and intrapersonal. According to Gardner, all people possess the eight intelligences in varying degrees, often with one or two of the intelligences being particularly strong. Mozart was high in musical intelligence, Picasso in spatial intelligence, and Fischer in spatial and logical intelligence. Introspective writer Virginia Woolf was high in linguistic and intrapersonal intelligence, Martha Graham and Tiger Woods in bodily kinesthetic intelligence, Gandhi in interpersonal intelligence, and Darwin in natural intelligence. Extending the rubber band theory, people have not one rubber band but eight, all in varying sizes.

According to Gardner (1998), the sizes of those eight bands or intelligences are a product of heredity and environment. As was true for general intelligence, heredity sets the band's initial size, and environment does the stretching. Gardner (1998) believes we are best served if we pursue activities and careers where we have a biological advantage or leverage. Mozart was well equipped for music and Picasso for art. Had each worked as hard in the other's domain, each might have been well accomplished, but it's unlikely that Mozart could have been Picasso or Picasso been Mozart. Although all eight rubber bands are stretchable, heredity puts us at an advantage in just some areas and even at a deficit in others.

So is talent born or made? Before answering, let's first confirm what talent is and is not. Talent is not potential but productivity, not promise but fulfillment, and not answers on an intelligence test but real-world achievement. Many have the potential to excel; few realize that potential. We know Mozart had musical talent not because of a test score but because he composed *The Marriage of Figaro* and the *Jupiter* symphony. As to whether talent is born or made, talent is largely made. Although heredity provides leverage in certain areas, talent rises only when certain environmental factors prevail. We next turn our attention to the environmental factors most associated with talent development.

ENVIRONMENTAL FACTORS IN TALENT DEVELOPMENT

Psychologist Benjamin Bloom (1985) studied the 120 most talented American adults in six domains: piano (music), sculpture (art), swimming, tennis, mathematics, and neurology. His purpose was to understand how childhood factors shaped talent development. Bloom interviewed the talented Americans along with their parents and teachers. Howard Gardner (1993) investigated eight extraordinary creators from the early 1900s, such as Mozart and Picasso, by examining their biographies. He searched for environmental commonalities in the creators' youth that explained their talent roots. My colleagues and I (Kiewra, O'Connor, McCrudden, & Liu, 2006) investigated young chess masters—children under age 16 who had attained a master rating. At the time of our study, just 1% of all chess players were masters, and there were just eight young masters in the United States—all of whom were boys. We interviewed the parents of six young masters to uncover the environmental factors that spurred these chess kids to become so good so fast. I mention these three studies because all investigated early environmental factors related to talent development, and all revealed five common factors: early experience, practice, singleness of purpose, mentorship, and family commitment. Each factor is discussed in turn.

Early Environment

In some cases, those who become talented adults are born into the talent area. Mozart and Picasso (Gardner, 1993) are cases in point. Their fathers were accomplished musicians and artists, respectively. Some of the talented people Bloom (1985) studied were also born into households where the eventual talent domain was operative. Parents in these homes were proficient and passionate artists, musicians, or athletes, for example. The parent of a tennis player remarked, "We always kidded that our daughter woke up in a car bed, next to the tennis courts, hearing the ping-pong of tennis balls—that was one of the first sounds she recollects probably. . . . We belonged to a tennis club and played tennis all weekend" (p. 447). Among the young chess masters, three of the six were reared in homes where parents or family members already played and valued chess.

Even when children were not born into the talent area, most enjoyed an early introduction, a head start, and were soon immersed in the talent area. Among the young chess masters, for example, chess play began between the ages of three and nine and the average starting age was six. Three of the six young masters, by the way, were introduced to chess outside the home, either in school or clubs. Whether the child was born into the talent area or brought the talent area home, the child-centered family became immersed in the talent area. The parents supported the child's early interest and development by exploring the area, providing informal lessons, and accessing equipment and resources. As the child's interest intensified, so did the family's interest and involvement. They spent increasingly more time playing, practicing, and traveling to events to watch or participate. Families became so impassioned with the child's talent area that they soon saw themselves as tennis, music, or swimming families as the following parent remarks, reported by Bloom (1985, p. 462), reveal.

- "Most of our vacations were frankly tennis-oriented."
- "The whole family revolved around the music."
- "Swimming was our way of life. All our vacations and extra money went to swimming weekends—that was our recreation."

The early environment was also one that instilled values likely to sprout talent. The parents in Bloom's (1985) study modeled and advocated hard work and perfection. The parents were tireless workers. Even in the home, they filled their leisure time with constructive hobbies such as reading, carpentry, sports, music, or photography and spurned idle activities such as watching television. While pursuing these activities, they also modeled the values and mechanics of studying a domain, establishing priorities, and organizing time. The parents pursued perfection in their work and held their children to the same standards. If something's worth doing, they'd say, it's worth doing right. Whether parents monitored the child's homework, household chores, or practice in the talent domain, the expectation was always a job best done.

Practice

An enriched early environment might jump-start a child on the road to Carnegie Hall, but only practice, practice, and more practice can deliver him. Among the young chess masters, most practiced 10 to 20 hours a week. Not only did the young masters practice a lot each week, they did so over a long time period. On average, it took the young masters eight years and 8,000 practice hours to attain a master rating.

Bloom (1985), too, found that heavy practice loads distinguished the top American performers from others—including those with comparable genetic stuff. In many of the families Bloom studied, siblings enjoyed the same early experiences and enriched opportunities to excel. But in only a very few cases did a sibling even come close to the level of accomplishment as the talented sibling Bloom studied. This was true even though many parents reported that it was another child in the family who early on seemed to possess more talent and natural ability. The one who "made it" was the one who practiced the most.

Logging a lot of playing time is not the same as practice, however. According to Anders Ericsson (1996), an expert in expert performance, the number of chess games played or the time spent playing the piano are weak predictors of skill level compared with the amount of effortful practice. Ericsson defines effortful practice as practice for the purpose of improvement. It is focused, arduous, and intense; it requires full concentration and most likely occurs alone. It is not social or necessarily enjoyable. A classic study (Ericsson, Krampe, & Tesch-Romer, 1993) investigating effortful practice examined the practice routines of expert level musicians over a 15-year period. The musicians spanned four groups ranging in expertise from "professional" to "best experts" to "good experts" to "least accomplished experts," in descending order. Results showed that the four groups spent the same amount of time on music activities (experience) but varied in effortful practice. The professionals, for example, practiced alone for about 25 hours per week, three times more than the least accomplished experts. Weekly practice differences, of course, really add up over time. At age 20, the two best groups had spent over 10,000 hours on effortful practice compared with the lower groups, which had spent 8,000 (good experts) and 5,000 (least accomplished experts) hours.

Effortful practice becomes a matter of routine for the highly talented. These comments came from the talented pianists Bloom (1985, p. 485) studied:

- "I would get up and practice just like you would get up and wash your face in the morning. It was a very natural thing to do, and you just accepted it as something very normal."
- "When you're studying four or five years, habit has taken over quite strongly."
- "Christmas was the only day off."

There are plenty of stories about the effortful practice routines of childhood experts in training. Mozart, for example, practiced for three hours per day beginning at age three. By age six, he had logged more than 3,500 practice hours (see Wargo, 2006). No wonder he was so much more talented than anyone in his peer group. Eric lo Shih-kai was 13 when he became the youngest golfer to ever play in a PGA European Tour event. His daily practice routine looked like this: Jog to a park at 7:00 a.m. and practice approach shots until school; after school, spend five or six hours practicing golf drills—sometimes hitting 300 golf balls in a session (see Marshall, 2003). Julliard School of Music teacher Dorothy DeLay has made a living working with violin prodigies such as Itzhak Perlman. DeLay insists that her students practice a minimum of 5 hours a day, but most actually practice 10 to 12 hours daily (see Renaud, 2000).

Singleness of Purpose

Long and daily practice sessions and immersion in the talent area (e.g., lessons, competitions, and performances) leave the talented individual with little time for outside activities. Among the young chess masters (Kiewra et al., 2006), only two of the six had secondary interests—both in music. The others spent the bulk of their free time on chess. One parent remarked, "The extraordinary amount of time we put toward this one activity takes him out of a lot of fun and games. The kid gives up an enormous amount to dedicate himself to the sport the way he does" (p. 102). For some of the young chess masters, social relationships are limited by their chess focus. One parent commented, "Chess is a little bit reclusive if you're using a computer and not interacting with other people" (p. 102). The young masters also spent little time watching television. While the national average for children is four hours of television viewing per day, two chess kids watched no television, and the four others watched less than an hour per day. When parents were asked why their chess kids spent so much time practicing and why they sacrificed other pursuits to do so, parents' answers were unanimous. All credited the child's chess passion. One parent remarked:

> He is passionate about it . . . just thrilled by it. . . . It gives him a lot of joy and satisfaction . . . and he's not really happy when he's not (playing). . . . If someone were to take chess away from him, he just wouldn't be a complete person. . . . We once took chess away and he was miserable; it was like yanking the soul out. (p. 103)

Sticking with the chess theme, I once had the pleasure of meeting American grandmaster Patrick Wolff at a tournament in South Dakota. While he paced the room between moves, I seized the opportunity to question him. "My name is Ken Kiewra," I blurted. "I'm an educational psychologist interested in talent development, so I wanted to ask how you got to where you are today." "I flew from Boston to Sioux City and took a puddle jumper from there to Sioux Falls," he answered, eyeing me quizzically. After I apologized and rephrased, he told me that it was practice and passion that made him strong. From the time he was in elementary school, he awoke every day to study chess for several hours before going to school. Chess was his passion. Fellow grandmaster Maurice Ashley (Killigrew, 1999) also dedicates himself to chess because he enjoys studying chess.

Ashley says, "I think the process (of studying chess) is the most delicious part of the struggle . . . that part of chess, learning about chess, is just fabulous. . . . For me, the process is the joy" (pp. 341–342).

To many of us, such single-mindedness seems unnatural, unhealthy, and even dangerous. Still, a pinpoint focus is one hallmark of creative giants. Consider the sad fate of Mozart after age 30 (Gardner, 1997). He had married but not the woman he most craved. His mother died, and then his father died shortly thereafter. Mozart was not able to secure lasting employment. His most creative works were not well received. He was poor and begged for money. And his health was deteriorating. So his productivity naturally plummeted during this stressful period? Not at all; Mozart's productivity continued unabated. His dogged determinism and passion sustained him. Or consider Picasso whose life was filled with hardships and the untimely deaths of loved ones (Gardner, 1993). Still, Picasso fulfilled his passion and painted at a steady rate despite the maelstrom of despair that often engulfed him.

Perhaps motivation psychologists Dweck and Siegelman sum it up best when they say that talented individuals simply practice a lot, want to practice a lot, and like to practice a lot (see Wargo, 2006). Their hard work is not the product of pushy parents but the child's rage to learn. In most cases, parents don't push talented children; talented children push parents. They push for lessons, tournament fees, equipment, transportation, and parental time. So should parents push back and deny or limit a child's passion in hopes for a more balanced life? Maybe, but to do so might be tantamount to yanking out the soul.

Mentors

An early start, a lot of practice, and singleness of purpose are not sufficient for talent development. According to Bloom (1985), the budding star also needs proper instruction, often from a series of mentors, over a 10- to 15-year period. In the Bloom study, children commonly worked with three mentors, each of whom fulfilled successively more complex roles that matched the student's development. First mentors were perfect for children. They introduced children to the domain in playful ways. Learning was fun and like a game. First mentors also praised students, encouraged them, and displayed enthusiasm for learning about the domain. Eventually, the child outgrew the first mentor. The child's growing commitment and knowledge base led to a second mentor—often at the urging of the first. The second mentor was a technical expert, a perfectionist who emphasized precision and accuracy. These mentors worked only with outstanding students committed to the talent domain. They demanded a great deal of effortful practice—up to five hours a day. Finally, students sought a third mentor, a master teacher nationally recognized as one of the few elite teachers in the field. Master teachers commonly worked at universities or served as national coaches. They mentored only a handful of individuals fully committed to and capable of excelling in their domain. They helped students correct minor flaws, analyze their own performance, grasp the larger purpose and meaning of the domain, and develop a personal style.

All the young chess masters worked with mentors (Kiewra et al., 2006). One parent commenting on how the child's first teacher made chess enjoyable said, "He was a wonderful coach . . . he really got the kids to laugh and enjoy" (p. 101). The parent reported that the coach and student often ate jelly beans and watched cartoons before playing chess. Most young masters worked with mentors regularly from the age of 5. Oftentimes, instruction began with a national master and later shifted to a grandmaster (the highest titled players) as the player's strength and commitment increased. Players routinely took lessons for two hours per week. Some players had more limited and less regular instruction, however, because of the limited availability of qualified coaches in the geographic region.

Oftentimes, budding stars gravitate to centers of excellence to work with the best mentors and other budding stars (Gardner, 1993). Mozart and Freud gravitated to Vienna, Europe's intellectual hub. Picasso went to Paris, the center for the arts. Dancer Martha Graham sashayed from California to New York, the center for dance. Today, budding musicians head to New York's Julliard School of Music. Tennis prodigies flock to tennis academies such as Nick Bollettieri's Tennis Academy in Florida. And chess players gravitate to New York or to one of the elite college chess programs, such as the University of Texas at Dallas. It is in these centers that budding stars get the best instruction available and rub elbows with other young Turks grappling with a domain's cutting edge.

Family Commitment

Benjamin Bloom (1985) said it is not enough for the child to commit to the talent area; the family must as well. No child can attain mastery without the family's support. Families—particularly the parents—assume various supportive roles. They are managers, financiers, motivators, and emotional pillars. Moreover, they make sacrifices to foster the child's talent development.

Parents of talented youngsters assume a managerial role. They arrange and monitor lessons, plan practice and competition schedules, make travel arrangements, access materials, and accompany the child to events, many of which are across country or overseas. One chess parent nicely summed up the managerial role parents play: "My son calls me his agent. That's kind of what I feel like. I do all the planning and everything else and he just gets on the plane or in the car and we go" (Kiewra et al., 2006, p. 103).

As "manager," parents also remove obstacles that block talent development. The families in Bloom's (1985) study, for example, juggled family schedules to chauffeur the child to and from twice-daily workouts or to the nearby city for lessons. They arranged mealtimes to conform to practice schedules or postponed family activities that interfered with lessons. They made special arrangements when the child had to miss school for practice or competitions and sometimes accepted average work in school. Parents even excused the talented child from family chores. One of the pianists Bloom interviewed said, "I got out of a lot of chores. . . . I was really indulged because I was the pianist" (p. 484). One of the parents remarked,

> We did give him special privileges. . . . We didn't feel that he should have little chores around the house because it cut into his music time. When we realized he did have this talent, we let him have full reign of time and did not force him to do things that other children do. We realized that he was special and that he should not be asked to wash the car. (p. 484)

Overall, families made the pursuit of talent the top priority.

Chess parents paid a heavy financial price to develop their sons' chess talents. On average, families spent about $10,000 annually on lessons, study materials, and travel. Bloom (1985) reported that the cost of talent development rose dramatically as the youngster became more proficient. Families paid premium prices for top instructors, funded extensive travel for workouts and competitions, and purchased first-rate equipment such as grand pianos.

Although talented children are largely self-motivated, parents keep them on track by monitoring lessons and practice sessions, making sure that full effort is given and that talent is not wasted. I (Kiewra et al., 2006) asked chess parents if they push their children to perform at such a high level, and these comments best capture what they said:

- "A lot of parents make the mistake of pushing their child when he really doesn't love it . . . it's not good for the child, parents . . . or anybody. It creates a lot of misery. Parents have to realize when to back off and when to really get in there and pitch" (p. 104).
- "I've made a commitment to him that as long as he continues to work and grow and do his best in chess and other things he has going on, we'll use whatever resources we have to get him where he needs to go" (p. 104).
- "I've had some very proud moments being his parent . . . but if he said tomorrow, 'I don't want to do this anymore,' I would say, 'Okay, it's your shot'" (p. 104).

Parents also offer emotional support to help their talented children deal with the rigors and stumbles of high-level training and competition. One chess parent remarked,

I don't understand the game of chess very well . . . but I understand the psyche of winning and losing and pressure. . . . I just try
to keep him upbeat and let him know I'm there for him [during
tournament competition]. . . . They are just young kids and they
need a lot of support. We're not over the point yet where when he
loses he might be fighting back those tears as hard as he
can. . . . So he needs mom or dad there for him. (Kiewra et al.,
2006, p. 103–104)

Bloom (1985) reported that talent development dominated family life.
The family's supreme commitment to the talented child—in terms of time,
resources, and emotion—meant that other family members had to sacri-
fice. Money for the new family car was spent on piano lessons. Family
activities and vacations revolved around competitions in the talent area.
Families sometimes relocated or split into two households so that the talented child could benefit from high-quality instruction only available far
from home. And siblings sometimes received less attention and fewer
resources than the talented one. One chess parent admitted (Kiewra et al.,
2006), "We dedicate the most time to him" (p. 104). Another said,

We didn't really pursue some of our other child's interests because
a lot of time was spent on him and chess. If we hadn't been doing
chess activities, maybe we would have turned our focus and pursued more of [the other child's] activities. (p.104)

Why do parents make sacrifices and spend so much time, money, and
energy cultivating talent? The parents Bloom (1985) interviewed said that
the pursuit of talent development actually brought their families together
for a common good. One parent remarked that the talent area provided "a
common interest and a common goal. . . . It helped our family become a
family because we were spending all our time together" (p. 474). The chess
parents (Kiewra et al., 2006) were unanimous in their response. They love
their sons and they love their chess. One said, "Well, I knew he had talent
and I didn't want to see it wither. If you're really good in one thing, you're
very, very fortunate so I just wanted to encourage that in him. I was proud
of his skill. I just knew it gave him joy" (p. 104). Another remarked,
"Because he's my son and I love him and I want him to be whatever he can
be. And, if it happens to be chess . . . then that's what I want for him. I
want him to be happy" (p. 105).

I agree with Benjamin Bloom (1985) who concludes that family support
is a crucial piece of the talent development puzzle. It is indeed difficult to
imagine how talented children could have secured top mentors and
resources, traveled widely for competitions, practiced regularly in an
effortful manner, and developed a supreme commitment to achievement
without maximum parental guidance and support.

IMPLICATIONS FOR TALENT DEVELOPMENT

Bloom (1985) studied the most talented people across six domains and derived this promising conclusion: What any person in the world can learn, almost all persons can learn if provided with appropriate . . . conditions of learning. According to Bloom, the development of talent requires enormous motivation, much support from family, the best teachers and role models possible, much time, and a singleness of purpose and dedication (p. 538). Educators—teachers, coaches, mentors, and parents—can provide the appropriate conditions of learning that enable students to become extraordinary or at least more extraordinary. Here are some implications for talent development.

Parents Are the Prime Movers

It is unreasonable to think that schools can take the lead in talent development (Bloom, 1985). Schools have plenty on their plate trying to give a wide range of students a general education. Parents, meanwhile, have ample opportunity for talent development. Consider these figures (Campbell, 1995): During the course of a year, a child attends school 20% of the time, is asleep 30% of the time, and is awake in the home 50% of the time. Moreover, a school provides just 600 hours of academic instruction per year (about 3.25 hours per day over 180 days). Given these figures, a parent can provide 62% more instruction by working with the child just one hour per day throughout the year. Two hours of daily home instruction more than doubles instructional time.

This single daily hour, or two hours—provided by the parent, a mentor, or coach—can be used for talent development in an area such as chess, music, art, or tennis. The sad reality, though, is that children waste a lot of home time watching television—about three to four hours daily. Or they are hooked to other technology such as computers, iPods, cell phones, and game players. Journalist Bill Moyers aptly said, "Our children are being raised by appliances."

Schools, to a lesser degree, can also provide enrichment opportunities that spark or even nourish talent development. Many schools, for example, offer before- or after-school programs in nonacademic domains such as music, chess, art, dance, and athletics. Some schools also identify highly gifted students and provide them with daily mentors in conventional school subjects such as English, math, or science. Such programs are exemplary for linking students with mentors but are limited because general intelligence is the gate keeper and nonacademic talents are ignored. Such programs should select and instruct gifted students representing various intelligences.

Build Cognitive Apprenticeships

Throughout history, one of the best teaching–learning methods is the apprenticeship. A budding plumber, electrician, or cabinetmaker learns at the feet of an experienced tradesperson who models and describes the craft. The best apprenticeships are cognitive in nature, such that the mentor reveals his or her ongoing thinking and inner conversation (Bransford, Brown, & Cocking, 2000). A chess mentor, for example, should do more than point out strong and weak moves. He or she should think aloud while considering move possibilities, thereby allowing the pupil "inside the head" of the mentor. Cognitive apprenticeships teach students how to think like masters.

In my estimation, the single best way to develop talent is through cognitive apprenticeships—hooking students to experts who reveal their inner conversation. All educators, of course, can build cognitive apprenticeships with students. Educators who want students to study effectively for tests can model effective SOAR study practices and reveal their thinking as they do. Educators can also model writing techniques and reveal their inner conversation as they choose active verbs, maintain tense, and tighten sentences.

The cognitive apprenticeship can be expanded into a cognitive triangle when the parent "doubly instructs" the child as did most parents Bloom (1985) interviewed. Parents observed the child's weekly lessons with the mentor and then reinforced the mentor's techniques and inner conversation throughout daily practice sessions. This double instruction allowed the child to advance at a more rapid rate. Ideally, mentors, parents, and school personnel can work in tandem to "triple instruct" the student.

Build Early Success

Early success in a talent area brings two distinct advantages. First, early success raises self-efficacy—the belief one has special ability. For Bloom's kids, as self-efficacy increased, commitment to the talent area increased—most notably in increased practice time. It is important, though, that students believe success stems from effort rather than genetic ability. Effort attributions lead students to work hard. Native ability attributions lead students to coast and to let their chromosomes steer.

The second benefit of early success is the notion of accumulated advantages: Those who are initially successful have greater opportunities for future success. Bloom (1985) notes, for example, that the pianists he studied had early musical advantages in the home not available to most children. These earliest advantages gave them a head start in music, which led to other advantages such as early lessons and rapidly becoming top music students. Being a top student led to more teacher time, better teachers, and more opportunities to perform. These accumulated advantages, of course, led to higher musical self-efficacy and more practice. The rich got richer.

Play to a Child's Strengths

Psychologist Howard Gardner (1998), architect of the multiple intelligence theory, is often asked, "Is it best to shore up a child's weaknesses or to exploit strengths?" In other words, should adults try to round out a child or to feed a particular strength or passion? Should Mrs. Fischer have made sure that chess champion Bobby Fischer could sing and dance? Should the Woods family have spent less on greens fees and more on trumpet lessons? Gardner admits that this decision is a personal one based on personal values. Gardner's personal view, though, is that adults should play to a child's strengths.

Playing to strengths rather than smoothing rough edges might yield three advantages. The first advantage is global. The world will have more Mozarts, Picassos, and Gandhis—more extraordinary products and ideas. The next two advantages are personal. One is that the talented individual will be happy pursuing the passion, fulfilling the rage to learn. We heard one chess parent say that to deny this passion is like yanking out the soul. The other personal advantage is that the talented individual experiences and learns what it takes to excel in an area. This understanding can be generalized to other areas. I heard one chess player remark, "When I was in college I struggled with physics, but then said to myself, 'Hey, I've mastered chess. I can use the same skills and motivation to master physics.'"

It's Not as Far as It Looks

A child comes before a tribal leader for his initiation into adulthood. The boy must jump from a cliff. The leader nudges the boy toward the edge; the child peers downward and recoils in fear. The sage leader calmly says, "Go ahead and jump. It's not as far as it looks."

I interviewed leading educational psychologists about their rise to prominence (Kiewra & Creswell, 2000). When educational psychologist Michael Pressley was asked what he might tell graduate students hoping to become prominent researchers some day, his words echoed those of the tribal leader:

> If anybody had really told me when I was in graduate school that I'd be sitting where I am right now, I probably wouldn't have believed it, but in retrospect it isn't as far from there to here as I would have thought at the time. (p. 154)

Budding stars must not exaggerate the gap between themselves and their role models. Educators must ensure them that the path is difficult but passable. As Hayes (1985) discovered, we are just 10 or so years of intensive study away from making extraordinary contributions. It's not as far as it looks.

STRATEGY INSTRUCTION: TEACHING STUDENTS TO BECOME MORE EXTRAORDINARY

This chapter described the five conditions of learning typically associated with extraordinary people: (1) They are jump-started in the talent area through early exposure, (2) they engage in effortful practice daily over many years, (3) they are driven by a singleness of purpose and a passion for their talent area, (4) they work with a series of mentors perfect for their level of talent development, and (5) they have the full support of family. Even if all these conditions are met, there is no guarantee that a Mozart, Picasso, or Gandhi will emerge. Still, educators and parents who produce these conditions to whatever degree possible will, at the very least, help students become more extraordinary and soar further toward success.

As students are helped to become more extraordinary, they can also be taught strategies that produce extraordinary performance. Here is an example of a high school soccer coach teaching the strategy of accumulated advantages.

> "Kerry, you're an outstanding soccer player with a potential future in the game, but to get there you'll need to use the strategy of accumulated advantages. This means that you need to seek and gain advantages that can produce more advantages." (*Introduce the strategy*)
>
> "Our soccer program does not provide you enough opportunity or notoriety. We play just three months a year, we're an average team, and this is a football-crazed state. These are disadvantages; you need advantages." (*Sell the strategy*)
>
> "Here is how you might practice the accumulated-advantages strategy. You can contact Coach Miller who runs the city's club program. Coach Miller is a former soccer Olympian who really knows the game and is well connected in the national soccer community. If you make their traveling team, you'll have the advantages of playing and practicing year-round against top competition. You'll also have the opportunity to play with regional and national all-star teams. These advantages will make you a superior player and put you in position to earn a soccer scholarship at an elite Division I college. That advantage could pave the way to making the national Olympic team. That advantage, in turn, can pave the way to a soccer career." (*Perfect the strategy*)
>
> "The accumulated-advantages strategy can be used anytime you're looking to advance. In fact, let me now explain how taking Advanced Placement courses in high school can produce some big advantages down the line." (*Generalize the strategy*)

References

Anderson, R. G., & Biddle, W. B. (1975). On asking people questions about what they are reading. *Psychology of Learning and Motivation, 9,* 90–132.

Atkinson, R. C., & Raugh, M. R. (1975). An application of the mnemonic keyword method to the acquisition of a Russian vocabulary. *Journal of Experimental Psychology: Human Learning and Memory, 104,* 126–133.

Atkinson, R. K., Derry, S. D., Renkl, A., & Wortham, D. W. (2000). Learning from examples: Instructional principles from the worked examples research. *Review of Educational Research, 70,* 181–214.

Atkinson, R. K., Levin, J. R., Kiewra, K. A., Meyers, T., Kim, S., Atkinson, L., Renandya, W. A., & Hwang, Y. (1999). Matrix and mnemonic text-processing adjuncts: Comparing and combining their components. *Journal of Educational Psychology, 91,* 342–357.

Bloom, B. (1985). *Developing talent in young people.* New York: Ballantine Books.

Boker, J. (1974). Immediate and delayed retention effects of interspersing questions in written instructional passages. *Journal of Educational Psychology, 66,* 96–98.

Brady, F. (1989). *Bobby Fischer: Profile of a prodigy.* New York: Courier Dover.

Bransford, J. D. (1979). *Human cognition: Learning, understanding, and remembering.* Belmont, CA: Wadsworth.

Bransford, J. D., Brown, A. L., & Cocking, R. R. (Eds.). (2000). *How people learn: Brain, mind, experience, and school.* Washington, DC: National Academy Press.

Bretzing, B. H., & Kulhavy, R. W. (1981). Note taking and passage style. *Journal of Educational Psychology, 73,* 242–250.

Campbell, J. R. (1995). *Raising your child to be gifted.* Cambridge, MA: Brookline Books.

Carney, R. N., & Levin, J. R. (2000). Mnemonic instruction, with a focus on transfer. *Journal of Educational Psychology, 92,* 783–790.

Charles, C. M. (1992). *Building classroom discipline.* White Plains, NY: Longman.

Charness, N., Krampe, R., & Mayr, U. (1996). The role of practice and coaching in entrepreneurial skill domains: An international comparison of life-span chess skill acquisition. In K. A. Ericsson (Ed.), *The road to excellence: The acquisition of expert performance in the arts and sciences, sports and games* (pp. 51–80). Mahwah, NJ: Lawrence Erlbaum.

Cherry, E. C. (1953). Some experiments on the recognition of speech with one and two ears. *Journal of the Acoustical Society of America, 25,* 975–979.

Cognition and Technology Group at Vanderbilt. (1997). *The Jasper Project: Lessons in curriculum instruction, assessment, and professional development.* Mahwah, NJ: Erlbaum.

Cotton, K. (1988). *Instructional reinforcement* (Close-Up No. 3). Portland, OR: Northwest Regional Educational Laboratory.

Csikszentmihalyi, M. (1996). *Creativity: Flow and the psychology of discovery and invention.* New York: HarperCollins.

Dick, W., Carey, L., & Carey, J. O. (2005). *The systematic design of instruction.* Boston: Allyn & Bacon.

Durkin, D. (1979). What classroom observations reveal about reading comprehension instruction. *Reading Research Quarterly, 14,* 481–538.

Ericsson, K. A. (1996). The acquisition of expert performance: An introduction to some of the issues. In K. A. Ericsson (Ed.), *The road to excellence: The acquisition of expert performance in the arts and sciences, sports and games* (pp. 51–80). Mahwah, NJ: Erlbaum.

Ericsson, K. A. (2003). Exceptional memorizers: Made, not born. *Trends in Cognitive Sciences, 7,* 233–235.

Ericsson, K. A., Krampe, R. T., & Tesch-Romer, C. (1993). The role of deliberate practice in the acquisition of expert performance. *Psychological Review, 100,* 363–406.

Ericsson, K. A., & Polson, P. G. (1988). An experimental analysis of the mechanism of a memory skill. *Journal of Experimental Psychology: Learning, Memory, and Cognition, 14,* 305–316.

Evertson, C. M., & Weinstein, C. S. (Eds.). (2006). *Handbook of classroom management: Research, practice, and contemporary issues.* Mahwah, NJ: Erlbaum.

Gagne, R. E. (1985). *The conditions of learning.* New York: Holt, Rinehart &Winston.

Gardner, H. (1993). *Creating minds.* New York: Basic Books.

Gardner, H. (1997). *Extraordinary minds.* New York: Basic Books.

Gardner, H. (1998). *Howard Gardner in-depth: A companion video presentation to creativity and leadership.* Los Angeles: Into the Classroom Media.

Gibson, J., & Light, P. (1967, February 4). Intelligence among university scientists. *Nature, 213,* 441–443.

Gubbels, P. S. (1999). *College student studying: A collective case study.* Unpublished doctoral dissertation, University of Nebraska, Lincoln.

Hartley, J. (1976). Lecture handouts and student note taking. *Programmed Learning and Educational Technology, 13,* 58–64.

Hayes, J. R. (1985). Three problems in teaching general skills. In S. F. Chipman, J. W. Segal, & R. Glaser (Eds.), *Thinking and learning skills.* Vol. 2. *Research and open questions* (pp. 391–405). Hillsdale, NJ: Erlbaum.

Howe, M. J. (1970). Using students' notes to examine the role of the individual learner in acquiring meaningful subject matter. *Journal of Educational Research, 64,* 61–63.

Hundert, J. (1976). The effectiveness of reinforcement, response cost, and mixed programs on classroom behavior. *Journal of Applied Behavior Analysis, 9,* 107.

Joyce, B. R., Weil, M., & Calhoun, E. (2000). *Models of teaching* (6th ed.). Boston: Allyn & Bacon.

Kauffman, D. F., & Kiewra, K. A. (1999, April). *Indexing, extraction, and localization effects for learning from matrices, text and outlines.* Montreal, Canada: American Educational Research Association.

Kauffman, D. F., LeBow, R., Kiewra, K. A., & Igo, B. (2000). *All matrices are not created equal: How ordering matrix topics and categories affects learning*. New Orleans, LA: American Educational Research Association.

Kiewra, K. A. (1985a). Investigating note taking and review: A depth of processing alternative. *Educational Psychologist, 20,* 23–32.

Kiewra, K. A. (1985b). Learning from a lecture: An investigation of note taking, review, and attendance at a lecture. *Human Learning, 4,* 73–77.

Kiewra, K. A. (1985c). Students' note-taking behaviors and the efficacy of providing the instructor's notes for review. *Contemporary Educational Psychology, 10,* 378–386.

Kiewra, K. A. (1994). The matrix representation system: Orientation, research, theory and application. In J. Smart (Ed.), *Higher education: Handbook of theory and research.* New York: Agathon.

Kiewra, K. A., & Benton, S. L. (1988). The relationship between information-processing ability and note taking. *Contemporary Educational Psychology, 13,* 33–44.

Kiewra, K. A., Benton, S. L., Kim, S., Risch, N., & Christensen, M. (1995). Effects of note taking format and study technique on recall and relational performance. *Contemporary Educational Psychology, 20,* 172–187.

Kiewra, K. A., & Creswell, J. W. (2000). Conversations with three highly productive educational psychologists: Richard Anderson, Richard Mayer, and Michael Pressley. *Educational Psychology Review, 12,* 135–161.

Kiewra, K. A., & DuBois, N. F. (1998). *Learning to learn: Making the transition from student to lifelong learner.* Needham Heights, MA: Allyn & Bacon.

Kiewra, K. A., DuBois, N. F., Christian, D., McShane, A., Meyerhoffer, M., & Roskelley, D. (1991). Note taking functions and techniques. *Journal of Educational Psychology, 83,* 240–245.

Kiewra, K. A., & Gubbels, P. S. (1997). Are educational psychology courses educationally and psychologically sound? What textbooks and teachers say. *Educational Psychology Review, 9,* 121–149.

Kiewra, K. A., Kauffman, D. F., Robinson, D., DuBois, N., & Staley, R. K. (1999). Supplementing floundering text with adjunct displays. *Journal of Instructional Science, 27,* 373–401.

Kiewra, K. A., Mayer, R. E., Christensen, M., Kim, S., & Risch, N. (1991). Effects of repetition on recall and note taking: Strategies for learning from lectures. *Journal of Educational Psychology, 83,* 120–123.

Kiewra, K. A., O'Connor, T., McCrudden, M., & Liu, X. (2006). Developing young chess masters: A collective case study. In T. Redman (Ed.), *Chess in education: Essays from the Koltanowski conference* (pp. 98–108). Richardson, Chess Program at the University of Texas at Dallas.

Killigrew, B. (May 1999). Player of the month: Maurice Ashley. *Chess Life, 54*(5), 340–342.

King, A. (1989). Effects of self-questioning training on college students' comprehension of lectures. *Contemporary Educational Psychology, 14,* 1–16.

King, A. (1992). Comparison of self-questioning, summarizing, and note taking-review as strategies for learning from lectures. *American Educational Research Journal, 29,* 303–323.

Kounin, J. S. (1970). *Discipline and group management in classrooms.* New York: Holt, Rhinehart & Winston.

Ladas, H. (1980). Note taking on lectures: An information processing approach. *Educational Psychologist, 15,* 44–53.

Locke, E. A. (1977). An empirical study of lecture note taking among college students. *Journal of Educational Research, 77*, 93–99.

Lorayne, H. (1985). *Harry Lorayne's page-a-minute memory book.* New York: Ballantine Books.

Marshall, A. (2003, February 10). Small wonders. *Time.* Retrieved June 15, 2008, from http://www.time.com/time/asia/covers/501030217/story.html

Mayer, R. E. (1984). Aids to prose comprehension. *Educational Psychologist, 19*, 30–42.

Mayer, R. E. (1996). Learning strategies for making sense out of expository text: The SOI model for guiding three cognitive processes in knowledge construction. *Educational Psychology Review, 8*, 357–371.

Mayer, R. E. (1997). Multimedia learning: Are we asking the right questions? *Educational Psychologist, 32*, 1–19.

Moore, J. C. (1968). Cueing for selective note taking. *Journal of Experimental Education, 36*, 69–72.

Neisser, U. (1982). *Memory observed: Remembering in natural contexts.* San Francisco: W. H. Freeman.

Palmatier, R. A., & Bennet, J. M. (1974). Note-taking habits of college students. *Journal of Reading, 18*, 215–218.

Parker-Pope, T. (2007, December 31). Will your resolutions last until February? Message posted to http://well.blogs.nytimes.com/2007/12/31/will-your-resolutions-last-to-february/

Payne, D. G., Klin, C. M., Lampinen, J. M., Neuschatz, J. S., & Lindsay, D. S. (1999). Memory applied. In F. T. Durso, R. Nickerson, R. W. Schvaneveldt, S. T. Dumais, D. S. Lindsay, & M. T. H. Chi (Eds.), *The handbook of applied cognition* (pp. 83–113). New York: Wiley.

Pintrich, P. R., & Schunk, D. H. (1996). *Motivation in education.* Englewood Cliffs, NJ: Merrill Prentice Hall.

Premack, D. (1959). Toward empirical behavior laws: I. Positive reinforcement. *Psychological Review, 66*, 219–233.

Pressley, M., Symons, S., McDaniel, M. A., Snyder, B. L., & Turnure, J. E. (1988). Elaborative interrogation facilitates acquisition of confusing facts. *Journal of Educational Psychology, 80*, 268–278.

Pressley, M., Woloshyn, & Associates. (1995). *Cognitive strategy instruction that really improves children's academic performance.* Cambridge, MA: Brookline Books.

Pressley, M., Yokoi, L., Van Meter, P., Van Etten, S., & Freebern, G. (1997). Some of the reasons why preparing for exams is so hard: What can be done to make it easier? *Educational Psychology Review, 3*, 136–143.

Prochaska, J. O., Norcross, J. C., & DiClemente, C. C. (2002). *Changing for good.* New York: Quill.

Reilly, R. (2005, June 20). Strongest dad in the world. *Sports Illustrated.* p. 88.

Renaud, L. (2000, October 1). Child prodigies: A poisoned paradise? *La Scena Musicale, 6*(2). Retrieved June 15, 2008, from http://www.scena.org/lsm/sm6-2/poison-en.html

Robinson, D., & Kiewra, K. A. (1995). Visual argument: Graphic organizers are superior to outlines in improving learning from text. *Journal of Educational Psychology, 87*, 455–467.

Skinner, B. F. (1953). *Science and human behavior.* New York: Macmillan.

Strayer, D. L., Drews, F. A., & Johnston, W. A. (2003). Cell phone-induced failures of visual attention during simulated driving. *Journal of Experimental Psychology: Applied, 9*, 23–32.

Sulzer-Azaroff, B., & Mayer, G. R. (1977). *Applying behavior analysis procedures with children and youth.* New York: Holt, Rinehart & Winston.

Tennyson, R. D., & Cocchiarella, M. J. (1986). An empirically based instructional design theory for teaching concepts. *Review of Educational Research, 56,* 40–71.

Terman, L. M., & Oden, M. H. (1947*). Genetic studies of genius.* Vol. 4. *The gifted child grows up.* Stanford, CA: Stanford University Press.

Titsworth, S., & Kiewra, K. A. (2004). Organizational lecture cues and student note taking. *Contemporary Educational Psychology, 29,* 447–461.

Torff, B., & Sessions, D. N. (2005). Principals' perceptions of the causes of teacher effectiveness. *Journal of Educational psychology, 97,* 530–537.

Van Meter, P., Yokoi, L., & Pressley, M. (1994). College students' theory of note taking derived from their perceptions of note taking. *Journal of Educational Psychology, 86,* 323–338.

Wallis, C. (2006, March 19). The multitasking generation. *Time, 167*(13), 48–55.

Wargo, E. (2006, August). The myth of prodigy and why it matters. *Association for Psychological Science, 19*(8). Retrieved June 15, 2008, from http://www.psychologicalscience.org/observer/getArticle.cfm?id=2026

Zimmerman, B. J., Bonner, S., & Kovach, R. (1996). *Developing self-regulated learners: Beyond achievement to self-efficacy.* Washington, DC: American Psychological Association.

Index